The Other Islam

Christian witness
to mystical Muslims

First Edition

Ted Collins

Published by The Higher Path, Manchester.
https://thehigherpath.co.uk

Cover design, typesetting and internal graphics:
John Tromans X313 Design – www.x313.co.uk

British Library Cataloguing-in Publication Data

A catalogue record for this book is available from the British Library.

ISBN: 978-0-900828-97-3

Acknowledgements

A number of people have participated in bringing this book to completion. I am indebted to Steve Bell and Rob Scott who both gave informed input and Paul Beverley gave valuable input both as an interested layman and as an editor. Andrew Bowker's patient editorial work has been invaluable and my wife Jean has been patient with me and an encouragement throughout.

Contents

WHAT PEOPLE ARE SAYING

"Ted's book is like Goldilocks' porridge. It neither too long nor too short, neither too detailed nor too un-nuanced, and neither too theoretical nor too practical. It is just right. It can help someone who has many Muslim friends think Biblically and listen carefully to their friends, so that they can present Jesus the Messiah more fully to them. It can help someone who knows only a little of Islam to see that there is more going on among Muslim people than they may have thought, and should equip them for saying something about Jesus to Muslim people they meet. It has helped me to get behind some of the things I see and hear in East London, and so, hopefully, to fruitfully show how Jesus both challenges and meets Sufi Muslim people's deepest needs. I will also be using his insights in my teaching and training of others.

ROBERT SCOTT
Cross-cultural worker at St Helen's Bishopsgate and part-time Lecturer in Islamic Studies at Oak Hill Theological College".

Ted Collins' wonderfully written exploration on the nature, origins and expressions of Sufism is a much-needed resource as it provides balance to numerous Christian studies based on conventional perspectives of Islam. The effort is also very timely due to current Sufi resurgences observed in many parts of the world. Collins' admirably articulates how Sufism departs from more traditional 'text-based' Islam; examines Sufi developments in contemporary Britain; and offers helpful reflections on what Christ-centred 'good news' can be for Sufis. Though academically sound, the book is accessible to everyone interested in understanding and connecting more with Sufi friends and neighbours. I enthusiastically recommend this incisive and concise work.

DR L MAK
Lecturer in Islamic Studies, All Nations Christian College.

WHAT PEOPLE ARE SAYING

Here is an accessible exposition, based on personal experience as well as academic research, of major themes within the Islamic world of Sufism. British readers may be surprised to learn of the adherents of this tradition who are likely to be as much their neighbours as Muslims with other orientations. Collins writes sensitively, yet with spiritual awareness and longing for Christian witness to such friends to be appropriate.

BISHOP BILL MUSK
Author of The Unseen face of Islam and Touching the Soul of Islam.

For a long time, the serious teaching of the mystical side of Islam has been missing from our courses on Islam. It is a difficult subject, and I often feel that it is easier and safer to keep to the clear formulas that more conservative variants of Islam display. Therefore, this very readable and clear explanation of Sufism, the breadth of its expressions and the many challenges that it presents to Christians wishing to share the Good News with Muslim friends, is a timely addition to the growing library of Christian Islam-related literature. He explores different expressions of International Sufism around the world, but particular the growth of British sufi traditions, before giving helpful suggestions as to how Christians might witness to 'mystical Muslim' friends.

This is an important book, as I'm not aware of any other book dealing with this subject in this way, and commend it to you.

REV CANON DR PHIL RAWLINGS
Diocese of Manchester Interfaith Officer and co-Director, Manchester Centre for the Study of Christianity and Islam.

The Other Islam

IT WAS A WEEKDAY EVENING in northern England a couple of weeks before Christmas. The rain conspired with the darkness to make it difficult to find the right house in the quiet suburban street. Some houses had bright decorations in the windows, shining through the drizzle. Cars began to arrive and, in ones and twos, people pushed their way past the Range Rover parked in the drive to get into the warm, bright interior. Small children hopped from one foot to the other, giving little shrieks as familiar visitors arrived. Everyone was greeted with a smile as coats were taken, and each person was ushered into the front room.

"Is so-and-so coming?" "Think so. Said he was." "Might be a few minutes late though…" The hum of happy chat continued for a while until someone said, "It looks like we are 'it' for this evening." The children were told they could stay in if they could behave themselves. Home-printed A4 sheets bound with a clear plastic cover were handed out. With a clearing of the throat, a young man sporting beard and glasses opened the meeting.

The booklet contained a litany, a whole order of service. They read together the prayers and confessions, some with the ease of familiarity and others stumbling over words and phrases. Some had their eyes closed, betraying a certain intensity, while others looked slightly distracted. The father of the two little girls fidgeting on an armchair monitored them with his eyes, quelling them when they got too boisterous.

At the end of one section the leader gave out a page number and after a brief rustle of papers and a bit of throat clearing the service resumed. One young man was holding a phone on which he was following the text. Then a hymn was announced, and the room filled with hearty singing. This was followed by a second hymn. One hymn had the verse in English, the second had the chorus in English. Up to that point, the whole service had been in Arabic. None of those present were Arabs or even students of Arabic language, but the texts, the confessions, the acclamations - everything - had been in Arabic up to that point. The point was not to understand every word but to participate in something beyond themselves accessed through a sacred language. At the end, tea and cake were served.

"We meet like this once a week," said the leader, "because our shaykh instructed us to." Their shaykh was, and indeed is, a Syrian gentleman currently living in Morocco on account of the war in his homeland. They meet in the comfortable home of a young solicitor. The gathering differed from a church house group in a number of respects. One was that, apart from the small children, only men were present. Also, although the through-lounge was furnished with armchairs and sofas, the men all sat on the floor. The content of the material was, of course, markedly different from a Christian group. The phrase "There is no God but God" was repeated 99 times, as was the expression "I seek the forgiveness of Allah".

The meeting was also significantly different from what you would see at Friday prayer in a mosque. The group sat in a circle, facing each other, not in rows facing the front. There was no prostrating. Although worship was addressed to God, the person of Muhammad was also a major focus. They would vehemently deny any suggestion of worshipping Muhammad, but they explicitly address Muhammad as a living presence. The chorus of one of the hymns was addressed to Muhammad and went: "... on you I count to reach paradise. So, in this life and the hereafter guide me through the way and hold my hand." The other included the words "Muhammad I beseech you to look at me... guard my heart from all impure... with you by my side I will fear no one..."

This group is just one of several in the area, possibly the smallest of them, each following a different Sufi shaykh. The similarities with a good church home group are striking – warmth, familiarity, informality, a sense of belonging. There is an idea in circulation which suggests that what churches most need in order to draw people in, and to retain those that they have, is to have a community feel. For these Muslims, that is something which they already have. They are also aware of their need of a saviour, but think they already have one.

This is just one expression of the "other" Islam in the twenty-first century in the UK. I need to emphasise *just one expression* because it is but one example of a diverse movement with many different expressions. What might strike *us* is how this gathering resembles a church home group, but that is not what makes it Sufi.

The *other* implies a contrast to something known. Here we are talking about an aspect of Islam which the general Christian public is unaware of and, to be fair, is often absent from the textbooks and publicity produced by Muslims themselves. We are talking about Sufism. We should not run away with the idea that there is a second separate version of Islam, some kind of vegetarian option. The fabric of Islam actually contains more than one substance; it is just that we are accustomed to viewing it through a lens that misleads us.

Fundamentally we are going to talk about people who we pass on our streets, and explore what some of them actually believe and practise, and then how to share Christ with them. If you are someone who wants to see people reached for Christ, then it helps to understand where they are coming from. We will find that the lines are not drawn where we would expect them to be, and that is why you have a book in your hands, not a tract or an article. We are going to explore a world we did not know was there, but which is a living reality for many of the Muslims who live alongside us.

This book is not written for experts or academics but for ordinary, faithful Christians who want to understand their Muslim neighbours and share Christ with them.

Treat this book as a guided exploration of one very important aspect of Islam today.

Love, Love, Love.

"**WE SERVE GOD OUT OF LOVE AND GRATITUDE,** but you Muslims serve God out of a desire to earn acceptance and forgiveness," said my well-meaning friend, a vicar in the Church of England.

His Muslim friend frowned. "No, not at all. We serve God out of love. Loving God and loving our neighbours is what we are all about," he replied.

Why would his Muslim friend say such a thing? After all, we all *know* that Islam is harsh, legalistic and driven by fear, don't we? I remember being told as a young man preparing to serve in the Muslim world that Muslims know about judgement but not about salvation; they have religion but do not have a saviour. Others told me with all the assurance that comes with repeating a well-known fact: "There is no love in Islam."

With that in mind consider the first verse of this Muslim hymn:[1]

The love of Muhammad and his family
Is my true Religion, my reason to be.
And if, when I die, my sins are too many
The love of Muhammad will rescue me.

---

1   This song was written by Ali Elsayed and the title is The Love of Muhammad. The lyrics and music are easy to find on line performed by a variety of people.

The third verse goes on:

> *For Allah to love you, obey his command.*
> *It says, if you love me, then follow Muhammad.*
> *To follow Muhammad, you must love Muhammad,*
> *For how can you follow that which you don't love?*

At this point we might find ourselves thinking about the fury and hatred unleashed in Muhammad's name over the Danish cartoons, but the last verse runs like this:

> *If you love Muhammad, you must love everyone,*
> *For his light is truly inside everyone.*
> *He is the mercy sent to everyone.*
> *Only through love can we all be one.*

You must love everyone? And what does it mean that his light is *in* everyone? These are just some of the themes we will explore in this book. If you search YouTube for the song you will find it being sung in a variety of settings around the world. This song is sung by one kind of Sufi Muslim. There are many kinds of Sufi, and not all of them sing. They follow different teachers, belong to different networks, and perform different rituals.

Is all this peripheral to the real Islam? Not according to Shaykh Abdal Hakim Murad, who tweeted, "If all Muslims were Sufis, all people would be Muslims." Born Tim Winter, he is a Cambridge University academic who embraced Islam in his teens. In an interview published in 2014, he said, "The ultimate proof of the religion is the saints. They are the miraculous expressions of divine love and it is through them that we come to know the Prophet. The Prophet is not just the theory. He has always been a living part of Islam."[2]

---

2   Jonas Atlas, *Halal Monk*, (Yunus Publishing, 2014) 95.

Saints? Divine love? This vocabulary might surprise us, but would be quite familiar to those worshipping in the many UK mosques classified as Barelvi. They make up about 36% of mosque capacity in the UK according to BBC journalist Innes Bowen[3], and are defined by their commitment to a Sufi understanding of Islam. A further 3% are described as "other Sufi". That takes us up to nearly 40%. Then the Deobandi movement accounts for another 40% of mosque capacity. They are sometimes characterised as "anti-Sufi" by other Muslims, but they would describe themselves as reformed Sufis, rejecting what they see as deviant excesses picked up from Indian culture, but holding firm to core Sufi teachings. There are different ways of doing the maths, but allegiance to Sufi Islam is certainly not an obscure feature on the fringe of Islam, not in the UK, nor in the world in general.

At one level, Islam is a system of law and prescribed ritual. At another level, it is a series of political entities that have risen and fallen on the world stage. Neither of these describes the full world of Islam. Examining historic Islam through yet another set of lenses, we find a world of mystics, ascetics and luminaries who have played key roles throughout Islam's history, not as a separate sect but as a presence that is woven through its very fabric. Looking back over the sweep of history, we may find Muslim armies that conquered territory, but in many places, it was the Sufi missionaries that won the hearts of local people. As Christian scholar J S Trimingham put it, "[Sufism] is the inner doctrine of Islam, the underlying mystery of the Qur'an."[4]

This dimension of Islamic life, highly diverse in its manifestations, is what is known as Sufism. In the past, as Islam extended into cultures radically different from that of the Arab World, Sufi practitioners were often in the forefront of taking Islamic spirituality to the general population, often developing distinctive local forms without losing connection with the mainstream.

---

3   Innes Bowen, *Medina in Birmingham*, (London: Hurst & Co., 2014), 8.

4   J Spencer Trimingham, *The Sufi Orders in Islam* (Oxford: Oxford University Press, 1971).

We are not going to spend our time exploring the past; our focus is on the present, and understanding the people who live alongside us. In the small town in northern England where I live, in addition to the seven overtly Sufi mosques, I am also aware of four different Sufi movements made up of younger people. They are attending house groups, running charities and conducting mission. Sufism is huge and it is currently undergoing a revival. The outlook of Sufis is significantly different from that described in typical Christian books about Islam. That is why this book is needed.

So, what is Sufism?

CHRISTIANS OFTEN APPROACH SUFISM LIKE THIS. We know that Islam is about laws, control and prescribed worship. It is about fear and a remote, unknowable God. Then we hear about Sufi Islam being about love, seeking God and devotional songs in local languages, and so we say this can't be the real Islam. In so doing, we agree with the fundamentalists and radicals who have their own particular vision of Islam that denies the mystical side, but we are not necessarily agreeing with the majority of Muslims.

The problem is that Islam never was simply rules and regulations. That is the way we have been taught to see it because one strand of Islam, that of the professional scholars of Islamic law, emphasises that aspect in their struggle within Islam to get the law applied. They are like the Pharisees we meet in the New Testament, always trying to apply the law. But as Jesus showed, there was always more to the law than ticking every box, more to worship that mere compliance. In Islam, the scholars of law write things down and systematise the teachings, and then outsiders (like us) access this aspect of Islam relatively easily. We Westerners expect to find Islam expressed as a clear, neat system, and we assume that this formal, legal Islam is the real thing, and everything else must be deviant, corrupt or an import from somewhere else. That view may make sense to us, but it is informed by just a narrow strand of what really goes on within the Muslim world.

Islamic lore, the vast library of stories and sayings that surround the origins of Islam, provides a vast, complicated mass of material from which it is possible to construct a variety of *different* images of Islam and of Muhammad. Legal scholars, especially those sponsored by rulers, emphasise governance and right behaviour. Others trawl through the same material and find Muhammad the mystic, the man who meditated, the man who sought and found the presence of God, the man who showed compassion in ways that scandalised the legalists. You can draw out a picture of Muhammad as the noble warrior, gracious yet firm as a governor. On the other hand, you can equally well draw out from the same mass of sources the image of a man reluctant to enter conflict, who gave away his possessions and loved tranquillity. Muhammad is, and always has been, the model for Muslims. From the earliest days, there has been a variety of perspectives on what following his example entails.

What then is Sufism? Is it a sect? A dissenting doctrine? A single-issue group? These are all reasonable questions. We look for the right category to place it in. No, it is none of those things; it is rather a whole dimension of Islamic life and civilisation. Sufism is an umbrella term under which we find many movements, activities, organisations, leaders, shades of beliefs and devotional practices. It is not an alternative to Sunni Islam or to Shi'a Islam. It is a dimension of both.

THE INNER DIMENSION

Sufism is sometimes dubbed the inner dimension of Islam. In some of the major streams of Christianity, we find contemplatives. They affirm the same doctrines as others but they relate to those doctrines differently. They view living by faith in Christ, and indeed life as a whole, through a different set of lenses to other believers. They practise disciplines that are precious to them but which they feel no need to impose on others. Such a comparison gives us just a hint concerning how Sufism is related to Islam as a whole.

Let us approach from another angle. Textbooks, both ours and theirs, describe the basics of the religion of Islam in terms of the six beliefs and the five practices, often listed in two columns, before going on to unpack each item in detail. If you like, belief (Arabic *iman*) and practice (Arabic *deen*) represent two dimensions, essential to understanding the whole. The one cannot exist without the other. If you have ever read anything about Islam, you are probably aware that these two lists frame the standard description of what Islam is.

Not long ago, I was reading the memoir of a pioneer missionary, who we shall call Larry, who had lived for decades in the land of Mali in the region that extends along the edges of the Sahara. Living close to his Muslim neighbours, he noticed that their understanding of their religion did not match what he had learned in missionary training school. He took the bold step of asking their religious leader, their imam, to teach him about their religion. He wanted to understand it as they did. Right from the start, the imam spoke of the *three* dimensions, *islam* – submission, religious duties; *iman* – faith, right belief; and then the third *ihsan*. Well, he did not use the word "dimension". What he did was to quote an ancient text known as Hadeeth Jibreel.

A LITTLE HISTORY

Very briefly, according to the standard view of Islamic history – other views are also available – Muhammad came along speaking words from God, and his followers memorised them. Then he died, and his followers continued to spread the religion, passing on the verses they had memorised, called the Qur'an, even before they were put into a book. As the movement spread, many questions arose which were not addressed in the Qur'an, and so the companions recalled the things Muhammad had said and done as a basis for deciding what they should do. These sayings were preserved and passed on orally for well over a hundred years before they were written down and collected. This then became a body of literature known today as the Hadeeth.

The written Hadeeth collections, made from the eighth century onwards, hold vastly more content than the Qur'an. Each Hadeeth collection that was made rejected the vast majority of reported sayings available at that time. Although these collections were made *long* after the events – and this is vital to understand – Muslims believe that all Hadeeths which were officially classified as authentic are genuine accounts of what really happened in the days of Muhammad.

Hadeeth Jibreel is a story from these collections. It recalls how a mysterious visitor came to visit Muhammad and his companions. He is described as a man in pure white clothing and jet-black hair who came to them without a trace of travelling upon him. He was not recognised by those reporting the story. He is said to have sat down before Muhammad bracing his knees against his, resting his hands on his legs.

The visitor then said, "Muhammad, tell me about Islam." Muhammad replied, "Islam is to testify that there is no god but Allah and that Muhammad is the Messenger of Allah, and to perform the prayer, give zakat, fast in Ramadan, and perform the pilgrimage to the House if you can find a way."

The stranger replied, "You have spoken the truth." Then he said, "Tell me about true faith [*iman*]." Muhammad answered, "It is to believe in Allah, His angels, His inspired Books, His messengers, the Last Day, and in destiny, its good and evil."

"You have spoken the truth," the visitor replied. "Now tell me about the perfection of faith [*ihsan*]." Muhammad answered, "It is to worship Allah as if you see Him, and if you see Him not, He nevertheless sees you."

Then the visitor left. Muhammad asked his companions if they knew who the visitor was. They said they did not. He said, "It was Gabriel [Arabic Jibreel], who came to you to teach you your religion."[5]

---

5   Nowadays, English translations of the Hadeeth literature are available as online resources. This particular account is to be found in the collection known as Sahiih Muslim, reference 1:37, hadeeth 8.

In this reported dialogue, we see that the five required practices of Islam, the six beliefs and then "perfection of faith" (*ihsan*) are all listed as making up what the *religion consists of*. This makes the third element, *ihsan*, necessary to complete the other two – a third dimension of the one thing, if you like. Books about Islam tend to present only the first two. The third is taught and practised much more in the oral tradition. Sufis take the first two for granted but pursue the third. Sufism is relational in its emphasis rather than systematic, it is personal rather than legal, and it is spiritual rather than doctrinal. It is about a retuning of the heart and soul and, as the account goes, worshipping God as though you see him. This is a text that many Sufi teachers go to as a descriptor of true Islam, the practices, the beliefs plus this inner quality.

Reading Larry's account, I was reminded of a time when I was a guest in a class taking place in Bradford, England. A Muslim prison chaplain of Pakistani heritage had been invited to help a group of adult Christian students to understand Islam. He was asked to speak about the beliefs and practices which he did. Then he went on to talk about worshiping as a Sufi Muslim. The first thing he explained is that *ihsan* is the necessary third dimension. Some time later, I was doing some research and was reading a booklet written by an American, Nuh Keller, who had become a Muslim as a young man and had gone on to become an Islamic scholar of some renown, living in the Middle East. When he was asked whether Sufism was an add-on to Islam, his response was to recount Hadeeth Jibreel. An African imam in the desert, a Pakistani chaplain in the UK and an American scholar in the Middle East, voices from different parts of the Muslim world all saying the same thing. Each one used this account in their presentation of what saw they as the basics of what Islam was, yet we do not find it in our standard textbooks about Islam.

A PATH

It's not that Sufism arose as an attempt to give substance to this story. Rather, those on the Sufi path within Islam look back to it as incontrovertible evidence that *real* Islam has always been more than assenting to the beliefs and performing the pillars. Sufism is here understood as the pursuit of ihsan. Using the Arabic term for Sufism, *tasawwuf*, Keller puts it this way. "*Tasawwuf* requires Islam through submission to the rules of Sacred Law. But Islam, for its part, equally requires *tasawwuf*." (Italics and capitals original).[6]

Sufism is described as a path, something that people intentionally enter and then move forward upon. It is not a set of convictions that one arrives at or a set of rules that one agrees to. Sufis are on a journey. That idea of a journey arises from a particular view of the world.

Muslims enter the Sufi path to learn how to worship God as though they see him. They know that something needs to change within them, and that they will need help from people further along the path. One ardent Sufi of my acquaintance put it like this. "The Qur'an is like a bank card. My shaykh has the pin number." Human effort is necessary but never enough. They know they need more than they have in themselves. Their understanding of the world allows for God to bless and favour some individuals and grant them spiritual wealth to share with others. It makes sense that in a hostile, unclean world, one should draw near to those who are closer to God in order to move forward themselves.

Sufis seek to be more aware of God by practising a set of disciplines in submission to a spiritual master. The master progressively initiates them into another kind of knowledge, a knowledge that is personal and relational rather than merely factual. In Arabic, they use two different words for knowledge. Knowledge from books and study is *Ilm*; knowledge gained through experience and relationship is *ma'arifa*. The spiritual masters, called shaykhs or *pirs*, train up disciples, teaching them to truly know, and to appoint successors who will carry on their work and make disciples themselves.

---

6   Nuh Keller. *Sufism and Islam*, Amman: Dar alFath, 2002, 14.

Because the role of the shaykh is so pivotal, over the centuries you get a branching effect (Figure 1). Within any particular tradition, an especially charismatic shaykh may arise. He is acclaimed by his followers and a sub-branch arises within that tradition.

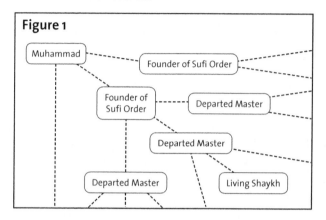

Figure 1

The shaykh ministers out of his relationship with God, as mediated through Muhammad. Although formal Islam denies that there can be any fresh revelation, shaykhs teach fresh interpretations behind closed doors to their intimate followers. They impart what they have learned from and through their masters and from visions of Muhammad. The outsider might view this as revelation by another name, but the followers of Sufism refuse to see it this way. There is a powerful conviction that much valuable knowledge is hidden. The formal scholars may grasp the surface-level knowledge of the Qur'an through their studies, but the hidden meaning has been passed down from one spiritual master to another, right from the beginning, and those who are truly enlightened perceive so much more than the mere scholar.

Those of a more text-based tradition do, from time to time, denounce Sufi shaykhs precisely for setting themselves up as new prophets. Reformists curb what they reckon to be excesses with varying degrees of success, and this leads to a creative interaction between the different traditions.

HOW MANY SUFIS?

Before we begin to think that we are getting this all pinned down, let's consider a different question. Which Muslims can be labelled as Sufi? How many of them are there? The question sounds simple but it is not. Ron Geaves, a secular professor of comparative religion, describes Sufism as being a set of concentric circles, and I am adapting his model.[7]

In Figure 2, we see the innermost circle, that of the Sufi masters, the ones who have advanced on the Sufi path and possess power and knowledge. These people are few in number. By one definition, these are the real Sufis. But Sufism is bigger than that. Around them is a larger, but still small, circle made up of those who have taken an oath of allegiance (*bay'ah*) to follow their master. Such a person is called a *mureed*. The *mureeds* vary in seniority. Senior *mureeds* may be authorised by the shaykh to teach and to initiate new members. Juniors *mureeds* may be complete beginners. All *mureeds* have committed themselves to submit to the shaykh and to obediently pursue the Sufi path under his guidance. The number of *mureeds* in any community is also not large.

Those in the next and much larger circle we might term "followers". I was recently at a special gathering that had been convened to host a visiting shaykh. I sat to one side of the room. A young Asian man was sitting next to me. I asked him if he was a *mureed*. "No," he said, "but whenever I get a chance to hear Shaykh Ibrahim, I take it." He was not committed, he had not pledged his allegiance, but he was serious. When doing my research, I spoke to several people who had paid attention to a variety of shaykhs for several years before arriving at a conviction that they should submit to one and become his *mureed*. The number of uncommitted followers is considerably larger than the numbers in the first two groups. This circle of people believe that the Sufi way is a real thing that demands their attention. It is part of their world, but their level of commitment is lower.

---

7   Ron Geaves & Theodore Gabriel, *Sufism in Britain* (London: Bloomsbury, 2015), 32.

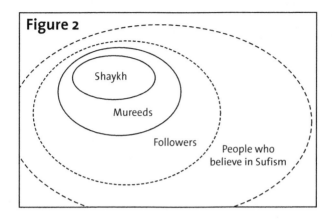

Figure 2

Shaykh

Mureeds

Followers

People who believe in Sufism

Outside that circle, is a much broader sweep of people for whom Sufism is simply a part of the complexity of their world. They don't doubt it, but they don't always believe all of it either. It is just part of the wallpaper of their lives. They may know people who are much more involved than themselves. These are people who turn to spiritual masters in time of crisis, and travel to the tombs of famous holy men, seeking proximity to God to meet a need.

For them, Sufi practitioners represent access to power, rather than simply teachers of spirituality. These people are not Sufis in the sense of being on the path, but Sufism is nevertheless part of their world, something that they believe to be authentic. This outer circle is very large. Some describe this level as *kismetic* religion. On the one hand, they have a profound belief in the power of fate, *kismet*, which is always beyond their power to change. On the other, they also believe that certain special individuals, Sufi masters, saints, do have the ability to change fate through their connectedness to the divine. It is a belief that they act upon. This circle embraces whole populations.

The idea of a single set of circles is, of course, a simplification. When we use it to map actual populations it becomes much more complex. There is never only one set of circles. There are multiple shaykhs of different standings each with their own set of followers. Some shaykhs are very tied to their location, others are not. Some have an international reach; others may operate within one neighbourhood. Some Sufi masters may be seen primarily as teachers of the way and others primarily as sources of divine power. Many operate in both ways to one degree or another. It is a complex and varied world.

The presence of Sufism is impossible to quantify, because those who believe in it are many and those that fully practice it are few, but both are part of the one whole.

There is an assumption in Western society that as science and rational education progress, all other ways of thinking must inevitably fade away. Anthropologist Katherine Ewing described working with highly educated and apparently secular people of Pakistani background, all dismissive of "traditional superstitions". They seemed to her no different in outlook to her Western students and colleagues. However, when she spoke to them of some strange encounters with Sufi masters, she would see a change in their demeanour, betraying a spiritual hunger and readiness to believe.[8] Despite their apparent adoption of a secular approach to life, the awareness of and belief in Sufism was still present. It only took one incident to bring it to the surface. How then can anyone do a headcount of people who believe in Sufism?

While Sufism is an important component of the Muslim world, it is not uncontested. Wahabism, the Saudi-style of Islam, bitterly opposes Sufism as a deviation from true Islam. The Saudis have been destroying historic Sufi sites in their own land and curbing the devotional use of historic sites. Few embrace the term Wahabi, even though they think the same way. Instead, many around the world call themselves *Salafi*, claiming to be returning to the ways of the original companions (*salaf*) of Muhammad. They are deeply suspicious if not openly hostile to Sufism.

---

8   Katherine P Ewing, *Arguing Sainthood*, (Durham and London: Duke University Press 1997).

In various times and places throughout history, there have been open conflicts between these different tendencies within Islam, but for the most part these varieties rub along together and interact. These conflicts arise from time to time precisely *because* the two tendencies normally exist in the same cultural space.

So that is the theory. What do Sufis do that is any different from the other Muslims? I am glad you asked.

What do Sufis actually *do*?

WALKING DOWN A NARROW STREET of African mud-brick houses, I could hear the rhythmical sound of a group of men chanting. As I passed a small neighbourhood mosque, also built of mud brick, I could see a group of men inside, sitting on mats roughly in a circle. In the centre was a white sheet, spread on the floor. They swayed slightly as they chanted *La ilah illa Allah* (there is no god but God), the first part of the Islamic creed. The leader used beads to count off the repetitions. The same phrase, over and over again. It had a melodious, hypnotic quality. This is one example of the practice of *zikir*.

When I lived in a town on the southern side of the Sahara, the Sufi chanting was part of the general soundscape. There were no regulations about noise, so some groups relayed their chanting through PA systems. Chanting and recitations of the Qur'an could go on all night through loudspeakers.

Although extremely varied in its forms, *zikir* is a universal characteristic of Sufism. You may also come across it spelled *dhikir*, *dhikr* or *dikir* and pronounced "zikir", "thikir" or "dikir", but it is the same thing and it means "remembrance". It is one of the key tools in pursuing *ihsan*, the perfection of faith and worshipping God as though you can see him. It is the most obvious manifestation of Sufi practice. It is the discipline of intentionally remembering the presence and greatness of God. Sufis see this practice as being in keeping with such Qur'anic verses instructing Muslims to remember Allah abundantly so that they might be successful (Q8:45) and telling them that the remembrance of Allah is the greatest deed, (Q29:45). You might reasonably describe it as a form of meditation, but traditionally we have tended to associate meditation with silence and stillness.

In the UK, where noise is much more regulated and the soundscape is full of other noise, *zikir* goes largely unnoticed. *Zikir* meetings take place in mosques, community halls and homes. There may well be a *zikir* circle near you.

In my African experience, *zikir* is usually performed by men, seated on the floor, without any musical instruments. I have witnessed similar but slightly different forms of *zikir* in the UK. I know a group of Sufis of Pakistani heritage following a Turkish shaykh who regularly chant those same words that I heard in Africa, but more melodiously and accompanied by a single drum. They have a chanting pattern that goes through other Islamic phrases, including the repetition of the single words Allah, *hayy* which means "living" and *hu* meaning "he is". The number of repetitions for each pattern is set by the shaykh and is rehearsed at their weekly gatherings. These are usually conducted seated on the floor. The group I have met locally meets weekly on Thursday evenings in the main mosque, and monthly on a Sunday afternoon in a hired community hall. Some groups are small enough to meet in homes, others are big enough to have bought a property.

As I say, the content of the *zikir* is determined by the shaykh, who prescribes it and authorises someone to lead it. Shaykh Yaqoubi, one of the current rising stars in international Sufism, prescribes a litany (the Sufi term is *wird*), which I have seen performed in a suburban living room. It includes the repetition of the phrase *istaghfar Allah*, which means "I seek the forgiveness of God" and *la ilah illa Allah*, there is no god but God, 100 times in each session. However, that particular shaykh goes further in his teaching. He recommends that each person makes this 100-fold repetition three times a day in their homes or workplaces[9]. This advice is not some personal whim, but is rooted in a long-established tradition developed in North Africa and the Middle East, the branch of Sufism which goes by the name *Shadhiliya.*

SHIMMERING LIGHT AND PIZZA

I know of another group, following a different tradition, which meets once a week in a hall above a dry cleaner's shop. They follow a Yemeni shaykh. Their litany takes about 45 minutes and is sung in Arabic. The hall is partitioned with curtains, and the women sit the other side but join in. They are mainly married couples with children. The litany is called the Shimmering Light and it is a weekly celebration of the birth of Muhammad. It includes repetitions, incense and the eating of a date.

The standard worship in the mosque has people standing in straight lines, bowing and repeating in unison, everyone facing the front. The prayer leader, the *imam*, has his back to the worshippers. Everything is anonymous. There is no interaction between the worshipers. Each person finds a space to occupy and goes through the cycle of actions and words without any reference to those around them. Many leave abruptly at the end without anything more than cursory greetings to those they pass on the way. The Sufi gatherings that I have been describing supplement the standard worship with something of a different quality. While I cannot speak for every tradition everywhere, all those I know of sit facing each other. They are groups of people who know each other and have a shared understanding. They usually eat together. Some have a pizza delivery timed to arrive as they are finishing. Some have younger members "learning to be servants" who go off and prepare a meal and then wait on the assembly.

While what I have seen is adapted to the British scene, it is firmly rooted in the traditions of Sufism. Elsewhere, in places where Sufi masters

---

9   Quoted from a brief YouTube clip. https://www.youtube.com/watch?v=u4r0MtPNEMI or https://bit.ly/32x49zz

hold court at massive pilgrimage centres, everyone is fed by the bounty of the shaykh. Pilgrims bring gifts, and the shaykh and his entourage run a hospitality programme.

For local groups, eating together is characteristic of the relational dimension of Sufism. They come together as a sort of family, a fellowship you might say. They may go on outings together. A group I know has recently gone away for a weekend of hill walking, and for a two-week trip together to visit historic Islamic sites in Central Asia. Such groups are likely to attend conferences together. They are all travellers on the same path, helping each other along. Does it sound a bit like a house church? Well, it is.

SINGING AND DANCING

Another feature of the three groups I have had opportunities to observe closely is that they sing. The ritual chanting itself is often musical, but they also sing what can only be called hymns. Usually part of the hymn is in Arabic, perhaps a familiar devotional phrase, but the rest is in English. It may be sung by the whole group or by a soloist. These are contemporary UK-based groups.

In the Indian subcontinent, they have songs – called *na't* – in Urdu, Punjabi, Bengali and other languages. They have a whole musical genre called *qawwali*. Professional and amateur *qawwali* singers abound. Devotional poetry (whether put to music or not) has been a feature of Middle Eastern Islam since the earliest times. While extremist groups like the Taliban became famous for banning all forms of music, pious Sufi Muslims celebrate their faith in poetry and song.

Another important variant of *zikir* is *sama'*. This literally means "listening", and is applied to the use of music and movement to enhance awareness. One form of *sama'* is very well known but is not usually recognised as a devotional practice. I am referring to the whirling dervishes. Turkey advertises them as a tourist attraction. A highly visual spectacle, accompanied by music, it is easily mistaken for entertainment, but a dervish is a devotee. The white cloaks and trousers, the belts and the tall earth-coloured hats are packed with symbolism. The practitioner is intentionally disconnecting from the everyday world and seeking to connect with the divine. The hat represents a tombstone, and the white clothing symbolises a shroud, for as I once heard a dervish master explain, "When we are aware of death, then we most value life." There is of course more to it than that. It is about dying to self and being lost in the presence of God.

Whirling is most closely associated with the Mevlevi tradition founded by Rumi, whose fame and media presence extends far beyond Sufism. Rumi was an Islamic Sufi master, and we shall say more about him in a later chapter.

We have seen that *zikir* can be public or private. There are forms requiring the participants to sit, others that require them to stand, and still others that require movement. *Zikir* can also be silent. In Africa, I often saw individual Muslims – who might at other times be chanting as a group – silently reciting as they work through way through their prayer beads. The introduction of silent *zikir* was a key factor in broadening the practice of Sufism in the Medieval period. Instead of disciples having to abandon normal life to spend time in the presence of a master, they could practise awareness in their places of work and in their homes.

Whirling is not the only form of *zikir* that combines chanting with movement. The *hadra* is performed in large groups. They harness those feelings that get stirred when people come together in a large, emotionally charged mass. *Hadra* events have much more vigorous movements. I have seen footage of middle-aged men literally jumping up and down on the spot. The recording was not made by some investigative reporter, exposing the eccentricities of mad Muslims; no, they are featured on Sufi sites. Try searches on YouTube for "Hadra sufi shaykh" and see what you find. There is so much more going on in Islam than our textbooks tell us.

One might reasonably ask how it is that there is such a variety of practice. After all, Islam is well known for looking pretty much the same all over the world, and every Islamic movement must, of necessity, claim to be rooted in the life and practice of Muhammad and his immediate companions. The answer lies in the other great Sufi universal, the shaykh, which we will come to soon. First, let's do some history.

Where did Sufism come from?

NOT EVERYONE ENJOYS HISTORY, but we do get curious about where things come from, don't we? If history is not your thing, feel free to skip ahead to the next chapter. You can always come back to this later.

One popular explanation for the origin of Sufism runs like this: *Islam emerged as dry legalistic religion that commanded an outward form of worship, but since this did not address the needs of the human heart, deviations began to emerge. As a result, elements of Gnosticism, Christian mysticism and, in the East, Hinduism crept in and contaminated Islam.*

This view makes a kind of sense. Scholars looking *from the outside* see elements that resemble what is found in other religious traditions. As worshippers of God ourselves, we take the view that mere outward observance is never satisfying to the human heart. There is a certain complacent satisfaction that comes from understanding the failings of others and being able to pigeonhole other people's experiences.

However, I have several problems with this view. For a start, I know devout conservative Muslims who repudiate Sufism and regard themselves as fulfilled and passionate about their faith. Their testimony undermines the notion that text-based Islam is simply a legalistic shell and outward conformity. But we shall continue on our track of making sense of Sufism.

Very few of us have investigated the history of Islam from the original sources. Christians tend to rely on the summarised accounts made easily available to us by others. Virtually everything we think we know about early Islam does originally come from Muslim sources. Both Christian and secular historians sift and interpret the data, but essentially we are all examining what Muslims say about themselves. What our abbreviated histories do not usually emphasise is the extent of our ignorance. There are significant gaps in the record on which we have to depend. This is not some kind of conspiracy theory; the fact is there are big gaps in the record. So, for example, historians might be quoted as saying that Sufism arose in the eleventh century, but what they actually mean is that written Sufi manuals started appearing at that time. The manuals themselves claim to refer to teachings and practices going back to the earliest days of Islam, but hard data on the earliest days of Islam simply do not exist.

Muhammad died in the year 632. According to the orthodox Islamic version, the Qur'an as we now have it was heard and memorised by a body of believers but not written down or collected together during Muhammad's lifetime. It is said that a concerted effort to collate and write it all down in a single volume was made about twenty years later, and a handful of copies were made. All Qur'ans today, it is claimed, are copies of that original. We have plenty of reasons to question that[10] – even drawing on Islamic sources – but from the point of view of discovering Islam's history it does not matter much one way or the other. The Qur'an contains very little narrative. It is not like the Bible with its built-in sacred history. It contains statements in poetic style, warnings, exhortations and commands, but it does not attempt to recount what happened in Muhammad's day.

---

10   A number of Christian writers have written trenchant accounts of the composition of the Qur'an, primarily with the intent of discrediting it. For a scholarly and impartial study, see Keith Small, *Holy Books have a History*. Kansas City: Avant Ministries, 2018.

WORD OF MOUTH

Following Muhammad's death, there was a period of about two hundred years from which we have no written records. The first document we know about that offered us any history was Ibn Ishaq's *seera* (sacred biography) of Muhammad. He wrote more than a hundred years after Muhammad's death, and no copies of his original work remain. What we do have is Ibn Hisham's *Seera* which is a revision of Ibn Ishaq's work produced later still. He was quite open about his editing role, and the version we have of Ibn Hisham's work was also edited by *his* followers. The result is that the oldest historical record we have comes from documents compiled a good two hundred years after the events. In those days, both in the Christian world and in the Muslim world, historical accuracy was only one of several considerations. The aim was to inform and edify the reader. Ibn Hisham was writing in the early 800s. His *Seera* is composed of stories and reports attributed to various oral sources, often contradicting each other in the details. He did not presume to decide which were true. In those days, ambiguity and uncertainty were seen as a positive sign of humility in the face of truth that only God could know for sure. The practice of *seera* writing continues to this day. Over the centuries, the accounts have become streamlined and idealised. Most accounts in circulation are intended to elicit veneration for Muhammad, not to give historical understanding. Ibn Hisham's work can easily be found online in PDF format. For a very readable history of *seera* writing, I recommend Tarif Khalid's *Portraits of Muhammad* for an overview of how biographies of Muhammad have changed over time.[11]

Back to our story. For about two hundred years following Muhammad's death, various accounts were passed on orally. The Muslim world extended from Spain to Pakistan and from Syria down to Tanzania. The teachings, practices and history of Islam were passed on by self-appointed teachers. The divide between Sunni and Shi'a Islam had at its heart a dispute about

---

11   Tarif Khalid, *Images of Muhammad*. (New York: Doubleday, 2009).

what had or had not taken place. In the early centuries, their competing versions of Islam's history were debated throughout the Muslim world, alongside other less well-known variants.

The *seera* and *hadeeth* collectors had to sift the oral accounts and determine what was authentic and what was not. And the written accounts that survive are those that had the patronage of the powerful behind them. One does not have to be paranoid to suspect that the accounts that have state backing are not necessarily telling the whole story. This means that even when we have some documents to work from, we have no reason to believe they even attempt to give a full account.

About the year 900, the Chinese technology of paper-making arrived in Baghdad, then the capital of the biggest Muslim state. It was only after the arrival of paper that written texts began to become a feature of Islamic civilisation, and even then, it took some time to become established. To this day, traditional Islam has a high oral component. The first explicitly Sufi documents only appeared after the idea of passing on information in writing had become established.

The tenth century was part of the golden age of Islamic civilisation. It is from this period that we can find a documentary record of serious debate about what did and did not make for good Islam. There was plenty to discuss. The diversity was great. Codification was on the agenda. The legal side of Islam began to take shape in this period, always striving to look back to the earliest years, via the oral tradition. Sufi codes and structures started to take shape in the same period, also looking back to the beginnings.

EARLY MYSTICS

Islam's first few centuries were turbulent. Looking back into that period, Sufis identify a number of individuals, mentioned in the standard histories, who embodied Sufism. These were usually people known for their pious devotion, who did not pursue power and wealth, in contrast to those who wielded political power. There was a strong ascetic dimension, repudiating the accumulation of wealth, seeking the comforts of the afterlife rather than the comforts of the present world. Such people attracted admirers. If you know your church history, you will spot parallels with the emergence of the Desert Fathers when Christianity became an imperial religion. The companions of Muhammad were reputed to be just such people, living simple lives of devotion, for whom worshipping God and following their prophet was the focus of their lives. The radical worshippers of the generations that followed saw themselves as following the example of Muhammad's companions.

Muhammad's role in the first community had been similar to that of Moses. He was the one who told people what God was saying. He was also seen as the best model to follow in everything that was not explicitly commanded. The community was dependent on what the companions said they remembered as a basis for addressing all kinds of questions. Islam as a political power spread very rapidly across a huge territory. It took with it a simple religious framework, that is to say, one God for all people, one messenger for all people, a call to righteous living and a pattern of worship. It also established a language, Arabic, as the vehicle for communication across the world.

Now, every location that Islam entered was populated by people who already had religious beliefs and practices. Many such populations already believed in the existence of one God and the importance of obeying his laws. They also had established ideas of what spirituality looked like. Some had elaborate theories about the spiritual universe. Their world was inhabited by monks, hermits, pilgrims, priests and saints. They venerated some places more than others, especially places associated with great holy people of the past. The essential message of Islam did not contradict any of these features of religious life; it just provided a new framework for organising them. Indeed, it would have been truly astonishing if people had simply wiped from their minds all they had ever known or thought in response to the spartan outline that formal Islam offered. Islam itself, right from the outset, acknowledged the existence of holy places, special messengers and levels of piety.

Speaking for myself, the existence of Sufi Islam needs no explanation. The diversity of spiritual expectation that existed already in the Arab world and beyond it found fresh expression under the new Islamic umbrella. The new Arabic-speaking cultural zone provided a space for interaction and development. Under Islam, the focus of these forms of spirituality was the unity of God and the uniqueness of his messenger.

WILD VARIETY

In the golden age of the tenth century, when Islam was being codified, we find lively debates going on about what was and was not appropriate to Islam. At that time, there seem to have been broadly two streams of Sufism, dubbed "Sober Sufism" and "Intoxicated Sufism". In both, worshippers sought union with God through the annihilation of the ego. The many and diverse advocates of the intoxicated variety saw the public outward expression of Islam as, at best, a stepping stone to the real encounter with God. Some of these would quite brazenly set aside the laws in the name of utter abandonment to God. Their poetry was emotive and even scandalous, evoking the recklessness of romantic infatuation. Not surprisingly, the authorities and their legal scholars were opposed to such threats to orderly life, and there are well-documented cases of persecution.[12]

The Sober Sufis also spoke the language of devotion, but stayed within the framework of laws and obligations, filling it with deeper meaning and seeking something beyond what mere book learning could ever supply. They too met with some hostility as they sought to serve higher ideals than governors required, and in so doing implicitly challenged the status quo. In the long run, the Sober Sufis eclipsed the Intoxicated, but tensions continued between the official state-backed forms of Islam and Sufi

---

12   One of the most famous Sufi martyrs, Mansur al-Hallaj, 858-922, was crucified.

practitioners. In the eleventh century, a man known as Imam Ghazali, a major scholar and intellectual of his day, abandoned state-sponsored Islam and embraced Sufism. After some time away from city life, he returned and wrote at length about how the different strands of Islam could and should work together. From that point onwards, Sufism became more accepted as part of mainstream Muslim society. It was still an area within which innovative charismatics emerged and also in which excesses occurred, but the heat generated by the rivalry between lawyers and mystics was dissipated. This is, it has to be said, an outrageous simplification, but it gives us a rough idea.

Over time, Sufism continued to develop in diversity with features such as wandering hermit-type individuals, small exclusive groups, mass popular movements, artisan confederations and, in some times and places, Sufi families ruling kingdoms.

RISE AND FALL?

One scheme for describing the history of Sufism runs like this. In the 7th–9th centuries, there were famous individuals whose piety drew the admiration of others. In the 10th–11th centuries, manuals of Sufi belief and practice started to circulate among the wider population. In the 12th–13th centuries Sufi organisations, often called brotherhoods, emerged with clear membership and structure. From the fourteenth century onwards, ways were found to make Sufism less elitist, making it possible for ordinary working people to participate. Sufi mystics played a major role in bringing ordinary people into practising Islam in many regions of the world. If you have a Muslim friend who comes from somewhere outside the Arab world, and you ask who it was that really established Islam in their part of the world, they will often name a Sufi – their equivalent of St Patrick.

By the eighteenth century, the story goes, Sufism entered a terminal decline, overwhelmed by the weight of myth and superstition, only valued by the ignorant and the desperate. This narrative, widely held and taught, is now breaking down. Sufism did not go into terminal decline; it is alive and vigorous today. That view also failed in that it implies that each stage *replaced* the previous one, whereas in fact there are still mystical individuals attracting admirers without necessarily forming groups of followers, and there are still new spiritual movements arising. *All* of the so-called evolutionary stages – the historic manifestations of Sufism – are still alive somewhere. Sufism has grown, developed and added layers. There are still individual hermits renouncing the world, and others who are engaged in religious empire building.

It is not the purpose of this book to give a complete history of Sufism. Our focus is on the Sufism we will meet on our streets and in our workplaces. We do not need to know "what really happened" or what is and what is not true Islam. What we do need to know is that Islam is very diverse. It consists of much more than the formulas described in our textbooks. We need to listen sympathetically to what our Muslim friends say they are about, and not simply reinterpret their words to fit into our own Christian framework.

Serious Sufis are seeking something deep, and if we as Christians want to respond to them, we need to embrace and celebrate the fullness that we have in Christ, not just be content with the outer trappings of our own faith.

The Sufi shaykh

"IT WAS MESMERIZING. I WAS MESMERIZED. I was sat in front of an old man, but to me he wasn't an old man. He was just a glowing emanating figure of light." These words were spoken by a young man I know who works in a call centre in northern England.

Here are some other voices. "He's like a guide, a guide to God which you can't get in books. You've got books, you know, there's a lot of guidance in books, but it's the shaykh who has actually reached God and he can say, 'Look, this is the way. Come follow me.'"

Speaking three years after Shaykh Nazim's death and quite deliberately speaking in the present tense, a *mureed* spoke to me of his shaykh using these words: "He comes and says things to me in my dreams that I need to do… When I'm in need of help, when I'm going through some trouble, sometimes I spiritually direct myself to him and I seem to get an answer."

All three speakers are people I have spoken with face to face. They were all born and raised in England. You might pass a person on the street today who talks in these terms. Some will ask how this can really be Islam. We will address that question, but first a few more quotes.

This story was quoted by researcher Rudiger Seesemann about the most famous African Sufi shaykh of the twentieth century, Ibrahim Niasse, who set up a community in Senegal and named it Medina and was referred to by his followers as *Baye* meaning father.

> On his way home from the market, a man carrying a bag full of meat passed by the mosque of Medina. As it was the time of the congregational prayer, he stopped and entered the mosque. Fearing that someone might steal the meat if he left it at the entrance, he took the bag inside and placed it next to his feet. Baye was leading the prayer, and after it was over, the man went home to prepare his meal. But to his great amazement, the meat remained raw; in fact, it did not change its consistency at all, as if it was not on the fire. Disturbed by this experience, he went to inform Baye about the incident. Baye listened patiently and responded: "Everything that is behind me in congregational prayer is immune against fire."[13]

Fire is shorthand for hell in the daily discourse of African Muslims. The story is circulated by his followers rather than by the shaykh himself. Whether any part the story has any basis in fact, we have no way of knowing, but miracle stories abound in societies that are influenced by Sufism. Let us not overlook the implications of this account. It presents the shaykh as a saviour. Those who follow him are immune from the fires of hell. The shaykh is not being presented in this account as a teacher or advisor; he is a living saviour.

How can this be Islam? Fundamental to all Muslim thinking is the idea of following "the example of the prophet". They understand him to have been specially chosen, to have been deeply pious, humble and in communion with God. We need to bear in mind that most Muslims grow up being told stories depicting Muhammad as an otherworldly, saintly character. Neither they nor their teachers have any interest in conducting a ruthless analysis of historical records, even Islamic ones. Very few go

---

13 Rudiger Seesemann. *The Divine Flood. Ibrahim Niasse and the Roots of a Twentieth-Century Sufi Revival.* (Oxford University Press 2011).

hunting through archives to seek out "hard facts". Why should they, when they *know* Muhammad was a wonderful man full of light and mercy?

In this context, one expectation that very easily arises is that some people, by following Muhammad's example closely, might in some way become like him, chosen, blessed, connected with God in a way that transcends nature. Their understanding of the divine economy makes room for such a possibility. That is what is believed of the greater shaykhs by their followers. The desire for special human leadership is understandable. The whole Shi'a branch of Islam teaches that God always intended Muhammad to be succeeded by blessed human beings, and that spiritual authority is always vested in a person chosen by God, rather than in books and legal formulations. This understanding and expectation can be traced back to Islam's earliest days, even if it was not always encouraged by those who actually had political power in their own hands. We could use another word, one more familiar to Christians. It is believed that certain people are given an anointing. Such people meet the needs of the believer in a more personal and direct way than mere books do.

From the earliest sources that we can access we find these two tracks: authority in laws and authority in special individuals. For those who prioritise the written records, it is about accessing the final revelation, given once and for all, and then applying it correctly in the present. For those who look for special individuals ordained by God, it is about identifying those truly equipped to model that same revelation and to unfold its implications.

For our convenience, we can separate them neatly into two camps, but in practice they are often intertwined. For many, a shaykh is the embodiment of Islam. Ordinary people often have no access to the meaning of the Qur'an, the intricacies of the legal system and the labyrinth of the *hadeeth* literature. But they do have their shaykh, a man emulating Muhammad, a man who speaks their language, an intermediary who has knowledge and has been chosen by God to guide the weak. He may be a fully trained scholar of the written materials or he may be a charismatic individual who ticks their boxes. Either way, he becomes the embodiment of Islam for his followers. To put it more crudely, he is their one-stop shop.

KNOWING AND REALLY KNOWING

The Arabic word *shaykh* is used in a variety of contexts to mean master, teacher, elder or governor. In Sufism, the term is used to refer to a person authorised to exercise spiritual authority and to take on disciples. In South Asia, Iran and Turkey the word *pir* is more often used to convey this same meaning. Seekers on the path sit at the feet of *pirs* or shaykhs, men who have travelled much further along the path than they themselves have or ever could. The teaching and practice of any shaykh has been learned from another recognised shaykh. The transmission is personal. They may or may not be a scholar of Islamic law, but Sufis recognise two kinds of knowledge. One is acquired via book learning. The other is *ma'arifa*, experiential knowledge, learned or imparted personally. To be a Sufi master and not simply a scholar, one must possess *ma'arifa*. To repeat the words of the man quoted at the top of this chapter, "there's a lot of guidance in books, but it's the shaykh who has actually reached God."

While the Qur'an remains the foundational text for Sufis, it is not the surface meaning that they prize. It is believed that there are multiple levels of meaning, and to access the deeper levels you need purity of heart and enlightenment. After all, in Islamic thinking the Qur'an is not a mere document, it is a manifestation of God's eternal power. It is foundational to Sufi thought that, in addition to the revelation written down and studied by scholars, Muhammad passed on secret teachings to those most worthy. These were then passed down orally from person to blessed person. Every Sufi master has a spiritual genealogy which they call *silsila* that goes all the way back to Muhammad.

In addition to this transmission of knowledge, it is understood that, as a Sufi practitioner rises above the frailties of his lower nature, he gains access to the spiritual realm. There he can receive instruction from long-departed saints and from Muhammad himself. Furthermore, chapter 18 of the Qur'an makes mention of an unnamed man who mentored Moses. Sufis call this man Khidir or Khizr. It is believed that this mysterious figure pops up through history to impart knowledge and guidance to the truly spiritual. He may come in a dream or in the form of a stranger. He figures in the spiritual biography of many Sufi masters.

Whatever we may make of all this, it does show that Sufi masters operate in a vibrant, living spiritual universe, not in a world of carefully argued legal texts. It is still an utterly Islamic world, just not the one we find in classic textbooks. The inner circle who pledge their full allegiance to a shaykh trust him implicitly as the mouthpiece of God. The story is told of a young man in Pakistan who had spent many years studying Islamic law and theology and then decided to approach a famous shaykh. The shaykh, known as Zindapir, who died in 2004, was not only a significant figure in twentieth century Pakistan, but he had a large following in the UK. This young student of law and theology said he wanted to become Zindapir's disciple, a *mureed*. Zindapir held up a piece of white cloth and said, "If I tell you it is black then you must accept it is black if you want to be my disciple." The young scholar agreed and took the oath. I give this example not because this is typical of all shaykhs but to indicate how little we understand of how things actually work in Islam.

THE AGE OF DIVINE REVELATION IS PASSED BUT...

The belief that revelation ceased with the death of Muhammad is fundamental to Islam. To suggest that anyone since Muhammad is a prophet receiving instruction from God is an absolute heresy for Muslims. It is unforgivable. For this very reason, the Ahmadi Muslims who follow a man who claimed to bring fresh revelation in the nineteenth century are denounced as dangerous deviants wherever they go, no matter how devout and faithful they are. However, as to the interpretation of that past revelation and the application of it to daily life, that is another thing. The revelation completed in the past can still be *a key to unlocking eternal realities in the present*, truths which were not explicitly stated in the text but were always intended to be unlocked by the enlightened. That is how Sufi teachers are able to bring fresh, living messages to their disciples.

We think of Muhammad as a historical figure whose legacy is treasured by his followers. For Sufis, Muhammad is an active presence. Yemeni shaykh Habib Umar al-Hafiz, one of the rising stars of international Sufism in the twenty-first century, is quoted as saying, "Someone who does not know Muhammad is alive is dead. When someone knows that Muhammad is alive his heart comes to life." One of his travelling representatives, Kadhim al-Saqqaf declared, "We never leave the presence of the Prophet. Did he not say, and he is most truthful – 'A man is with whom he loves.'"

The term "Barelvi" is used to describe the whole spectrum of pro-Sufi Islam in India and Pakistan. Belief that Muhammad is *hazir o nazir*, present and watching, is a cornerstone of Barelvi orthodoxy. The Barelvis account for about 36% of mosque capacity in the UK.[14] While other traditions may not see things in such stark terms, the belief that the higher shaykhs can be in communication with Muhammad is very widespread.

All this gives Sufi shaykhs a great ability to innovate. As many readers will be aware, innovation is one of the dirtiest words in Islamic theology. How, you might ask, do they get away with it? Many don't. Those who successfully draw disciples and lead them effectively grow in reputation and influence. Their success becomes their validation. They have to act wisely to retain credibility. By their fruits they are known. Their lives are constantly under scrutiny, and any failings can halt their progress. They operate in a contested environment. If they have enough personal charisma, they can build a following of people who trust them utterly. Then when they say, "This is the way, this is the secret little known, this is how

---

14 Innes Bowen, *Medina in Birmingham, Najaf in Brent – Inside British Islam* (London: Hurst & Co., 2014), 7.

the Prophet wants us to respond to these new challenges", their word is accepted without question.

It is in such a setting that they can instruct their followers how to pursue *ihsan*, the perfection of faith. They can instruct their followers in any and every area of life. The link is personal. They have no obligation to teach everyone the same thing. The whole process is relational and mystical.

THE POWER TO INNOVATE

A UK-based anthropologist of Balkan heritage, Dejan Azdajic, studied the work of two Sufi masters and their followers in Bosnia. The two belonged to the same Sufi tradition and operated in the same cultural environment. Azdajic found significant differences in the life and teachings of the two groups. He concluded that each group was shaped by the person and priorities of its shaykh. Given the autonomy of the shaykhs, it is not difficult to see how new traditions can be developed over time. It is probably no accident that, throughout history, great shaykhs have emerged at times when the Muslim world has been in a state of crisis and the conventional authorities have been thrown into disarray. Looking for certainty in times of insecurity, people often turn to those who plausibly embody the religion they believe in and speak into their current situation, rather than simply rummaging through ancient records and looking for something that might fit.

To be sure, there were and are movements within Islam that reject this whole view of the world and insist on the equality of all Muslims before God. That tendency was growing through the twentieth century. At the same time there are others who go so far as to put Sufi saints above and beyond the laws of Islam. They see regular Islam as merely the minimum level, intended for the common people, while God's chosen ones live at an utterly different level, wrapped in the divine loving presence. Islam is a world of diversity. But those that follow the Islam of saints and mystics look to Muhammad and the Qur'an as their source as much as anyone else.

This takes us into what the anthropologists call "worldview". Every culture has a way of seeing the world around them. The kind of world we believe ourselves to be living in shapes our assumptions and our expectations. In a secular, materialist world, people find it hard to believe in miracles, even when confronted with evidence. They expect to find rational explanations. Such explanations sound much more credible to them than the so-called supernatural events that occurred long ago, no matter how many witnesses might have seen them. The rational explanation is more satisfying precisely because it meets the expectations arising from their worldview.

BEING CONNECTED

For the ordinary follower the shaykh is a presence, not just a resource or a teacher. Truth is embodied in his person. The shaykh is an intermediary capable of giving authentic guidance and of accessing supernatural power. The follower's relationship to the shaykh is personal. One of the keys to advancing on the true path for the true seeker is called *suhba*, which means something like "keeping company". I have friends in the UK who travel at least once a year to spend time in the presence of their shaykh in Cyprus. They participate in worship and receive teaching. They go for walks on the beach and generally enjoy themselves, but part of that time, whether one to one or in small groups, is with their shaykh. Such times shape their year. The practice of *suhba* is also extended through authorised representatives – trainee shaykhs if you like – who may live in the UK or travel here regularly. *Suhba* also occurs when the shaykh himself travels and visits. Even without the shaykh's physical presence, when a group of followers gather together this too is an aspect of *suhba*.

The day that I wrote the paragraph above about *suhba*, I visited a friend who is an imam, in his office at the mosque. Among the leaflets and free literature on the rack was a notice about a conference coming up at which the top shaykh of their Sufi organisation was going to be the main speaker. However, the word "conference" was not used. A conference is an event at which people come to confer, to talk to each other. Nor was it a convention, an event where people come to be together. No, it was described as a *suhba* – an opportunity *to be in the presence of the shaykh*. The event was to be defined by his presence, not by the fact that people came to it.

Then there is the technical term, *rabita*. This word means a bond or a tie; not a mere link or connection, but a binding. The *mureed*, that is the follower who has taken the oath of allegiance, *is bound* to his or his shaykh. For such a person, there is a sense in which the shaykh is always present. They expect the shaykh to be aware of them and to be shaping their circumstances. Some shaykhs give their followers a personalised amulet to wear under their clothes 24/7. The idea of a living personal link is a very strong element for the *mureeds* in that inner circle of Sufism.

Here are some things committed Sufi followers have said in my presence:

"You have this spiritual connection is called *rabita*. That spiritual connection is you can call them from millions and millions of miles away and they will come just like that."

"If you have a shaykh – you know that they're watching you – in a sense they're connected with you."

"What we are taught is that [the shaykhs] will have some effect on you... just because of how spiritual they are, that will just have an effect on you. Whether you are making an active effort or not, it'll just have an effect."

These examples are the experience of individual committed followers. In more traditional settings, in Pakistan or Bangladesh, it may be a whole family that is bound to the shaykh. This brings us to a couple of other features of traditional Sufism. The thinking goes like this. If the shaykh is really a source of blessing to all around him, then the places he is associated with and his family are special too. Therefore Sufi masters are normally buried in the place where they conducted their ministry. In fact, it is customary for a shaykh with a big following to start building his tomb while he is still alive. People then continue to visit, to come into his presence, after the shaykh has died. His blessing lives on. It is understood to be a tangible presence. Furthermore, the sons of the shaykh inherit their father's legacy. In some traditions, notably in Asia, we find whole Sufi dynasties.

Those who are regarded as holy by virtue of their ancestry are called *sajjad nashin*. It is not unusual after a shaykh's death for there to be a discreet tussle over control of the shrine between his family and his most devoted followers, themselves trainee shaykhs. Of course, it is also possible for members of a shaykh's family to follow wholeheartedly the Sufi path, and attain all the attributes of shaykhdom such that they would be recognised even without their family connection, and some do. Others get the benefits of inheriting the status without walking the path. In these forward-looking days, shaykhs heading up large organisations prepare their sons to take up such a role.

This inheritance model makes it possible for a follower family to be bound to a shaykh through many generations because there is always a holy heir to maintain the covenant. It becomes a form of tribal affiliation. In this book, we are mainly interested in what is happening in the UK setting. Bonds to *sajjad nashin* do exist in the UK, but they tend to be backward looking, focussed on what was "in the home country". This nevertheless forms part of the background for those following the latest developments in Sufism that are flourishing in the twenty-first century.

Great Shaykhs

THE MOST PROMINENT MOSQUE IN THE TOWN where I now live is called the Ghausia Mosque. It has given birth to a second mosque of the same name, not half a mile away. We also have a small girls' school and several shops of that name. And down the road in the next town, there is another Ghausia Mosque. The name is taken from a title, *Ghaus-e-Azam*, which means something like "the great source of help", a title not ascribed to God but to a man, Shaykh Abdal-Qadir al-Jilani who lived 900 years ago. And to complete the picture, we also have a nearby Gilani Centre (different spelling of Jilani), the base of operations for one of his descendants. Several local businesses also incorporate Jilani/Gilani into their names.

Sufis look back to many great shaykhs of the past. To get a better understanding of the present, we are going to do a little more history. Each part of the Muslim world has its particular heroes. Here, we are going to meet just three major figures who are genuinely significant in history and also have a tangible legacy in the present. If you have a Muslim friend with an interest in Sufism, you might ask them what these names mean to them.

AL-JILANI, 1077–1166

Abd al-Qadir al-Jilani was a Persian born in Jilan (also spelled Gilan) in what is now Iran. He was sent to study in Baghdad, and later served as a teacher there. He grew up at the beginning of that period of history we know as the Crusades. Jilani was trained as an expert in Islamic law and theology, but on completing his formal education he went off seeking mystical knowledge, and spent 25 years in the desert. When he came back to Baghdad, he served as a teacher of both Islamic law and the inner life. He became known as a great orator and "renewer of religion" in that city. To use Christian terms, he brought revival to the populace at large. Backsliding and lawlessness were replaced by repentance and religious devotion. He is also said to have brought many Jews and Christians into Islam.

Fabulous miracles are attributed to him. Walking on water and the miraculous provision of food are modest examples in comparison with some of the others. There is a story that he picked up a book about philosophy, glanced through it and handed it back to its owner, who found it had been totally rewritten. It had become a book about Islam. There is another about him turning the bones of a chicken he had just eaten into a living bird which called out the Islamic confession of faith. There is yet another about how he caused a Christian priest, who admired Islam but would not embrace it, to experience in one moment a whole alternative life as a woman. When the moment passed, Jilani presented the priest with the adult sons whose mother he had been in that alternative life.[15]

The earliest known biography was written a hundred years after his death. Even in Medieval times some scholars ridiculed the miracles ascribed to him. Jilani lived at a time when people loved fabulous tales. They also believed that nothing was impossible for the man who truly overcame his lower self and attained union with God. The stories about his command over time and space reflect this underlying belief. In terms of his character, he is remembered as one who was gentle and kind, happy to associate with the poor, and unimpressed with the powerful. He was said to always speak the truth, and promoted a life of love, peace and serenity.

---

15 Abd al-Qadir al-Jilani, *Secret of Secrets*, trans. Shaykh Tosun al-Jerrahi al Halveti. Cambridge: The Islamic Texts Society 1992).

Up until his time, Sufism had been primarily associated with the lifestyle of special individuals. It was a spiritual path that individuals might choose to pursue. The followers of Jilani became an organisation, a 'tariqa'. From this point forward, people started entering the Sufi path by joining a tariqa. The word literally means 'path' but is often translated into English as "a brotherhood" or "order" – akin to monastic orders – precisely because it refers to a structured association of followers. The tariqa formed by the followers of Jilani is known as the Qadiriyya. It spread throughout the Islamic world and has given rise to various offshoots. Many a shaykh traces his spiritual ancestry back through Jilani.

Although Jilani is usually described as the founder of the Qadiriyya order, there is no evidence to suggest that he had any intention of starting a new organisation. Rather, his disciples created the order in his name, transmitted his teachings and built up his legacy. It might be truer to say that he inspired it rather than founded it. In this period other tariqas arose, each one founded or inspired by a great teacher or saint. Jilani is seen as the model Sufi master, and later would-be shaykhs have sought to emulate him.

The memory of Jilani is kept alive across the UK in many settings. He is commemorated in many Asian-led mosques at monthly and/or annual events called *Giarvin-e-shareef* (spellings vary). His legacy takes many forms. Whole networks look back to him as their inspiration. One is the Sultan Bahu Trust. Sultan Bahu was a seventeenth century shaykh who wrote devotional poetry in the Punjabi language and is revered to this day. The man himself was a follower of Jilani and a member of the Qadiriyya, and so the Sultan Bahu network is an offshoot of that group. It has several thriving mosques in the UK.

Minhaj-ul-Quran International (MQI) is a modern Sufi-inspired network, founded in 1981 by Pakistani Muhammad-Tahir-ul-Qadri. A friend of mine who is an MQI *imam* tells me they have 19 branches in the UK and plenty of others in Europe. The members of MQI see themselves as drawing on a Qadiriyya heritage. It is said that their founder, ul-Qadri, once had a dream in which he was told that all his followers would automatically come under the guidance of Abdal-Qadir al-Jilani.

Al-Jilani, or at least the account of him that has come down to us, serves as a template in the Sufi-leaning Muslim world for what a truly great man of God should look like.

IBN ARABI 1165–1240

The other day I was reading the Facebook page of an Englishman living in West Yorkshire who has not only become a Muslim but is now recognised as a Sufi shaykh. The first two posts both referred to Ibn Arabi, and to the view that everything in life is an expression of God's mercy. I have recently attended a major Sufi event packed with young adults, and there on the bookstalls for today's serious students of Sufism, are English translations of Ibn Arabi.

The name Ibn Arabi is totally unknown to most British people, but he was a towering figure who has had a huge impact across the world, and is still quoted by those involved with Sufism today.

Ibn Arabi was born in Muslim Spain. He did not receive any special religious education. His father was a secretary in the royal court, and Ibn Arabi grew up in constant contact with men of power and learning. In his teens, he is said to have received a vision which started him on a journey. He says that in these visions Jesus was his first guide. We do not know what transpired in his teens, but there is no particular evidence of the influence of Christ in his teachings.

From the age of 19, he started learning the ways of the Sufis. He also applied himself to other areas of Islamic knowledge. At the age of 30, he left Spain and went to Tunis, and five years later received a vision sending him further east. He spent time in a variety of important cities in the Muslim world, teaching and learning, before settling in the great city of Damascus. He was a prolific writer. About 850 works were attributed to him, of which at least 700 are probably authentic. Of these, 400 are still in circulation today. They include densely written books of theological philosophy and collections of devotional poetry.

Unlike most Sufi writers up to this point, he did not simply recount the tales of previous mystics or base his teaching on their words and deeds. Rather, he drew on Islamic knowledge as a whole and developed a whole system of his own for understanding God and the created world. He reasoned from familiar texts but also drew on his visionary experiences. He provided a sort of theoretical framework for all spiritual knowledge. He taught from the Qur'an – and about it – arguing that it had many levels of meaning.

Above all he taught about the nature of reality, that what we see on the surface is not what matters. Without the "removal of veils" the human mind cannot grasp any significant truth. In other words, without mystical experiences you cannot truly *know*. He argued that only God truly knows anything, and only God is truly worth knowing. A phrase like "he developed systems of understanding" tends to suggest that he made things simple, ordered and clear. Not at all. His writings are deeply frustrating for anyone looking for a sort of "Spiritual Truth for Dummies". Real knowledge had to be apprehended by the soul, not learned from books. He did not make it easy for anyone. In due course, scholars started writing commentaries on what he had written, each of which was vastly longer than the original. It is not that everyone agreed with him, but such was his impact that no scholar could ignore him.

He is most famous for propounding the doctrine known as *Wahdat al-Wujood*, usually translated as the "Unity of Being" or "Unity of Existence". Since all things come from God and are sustained by God, imagined and decreed by God, then, he reasoned, all reality is an expression of God. Only God is truly real. For Ibn Arabi, the world was constantly being recreated, it was vibrant and living, full of divine disclosure for those who could see it. He has been labelled by some as a pantheist but that would be a misreading. He always distinguished between God himself and the creation which comes from him.

In common with some Christian mystics of the age, he taught that the key to knowing God was to know one's self, for the soul is, in some way, the image of God. The business of true worshippers was to draw close to God, and have the reflection and presence of God suffusing themselves. That God's overriding characteristic is mercy was fundamental to Ibn Arabi. In English, we use the word "mercy" in a rather narrow sense, but in Arabic and especially for Ibn Arabi, mercy covers kindness, grace and total goodness. From Ibn Arabi's perspective, as worshippers begin to know God in their experience, they will love him and be drawn deeper into the awareness of God.

Although only serious scholars have grappled directly with the thought of Ibn Arabi, his writings have shaped the terminology of Sufism, affecting all the Sufi movements. His perceptions were transmitted across the world in poetry in Persian, Turkish and Urdu, so that his teachings permeated down deeply into the culture. Aspects of his thought were taken up in the songs and poetry of unwritten languages too. Secular academic Francis Robinson describes how the songs sung by women in rural India as they performed routine tasks such as grinding grain or rocking their babies were suffused with a Sufi understanding of the world.[16] The high intellectual reasoning of people like Ibn Arabi filtered down into every level of society.

RUMI 1207–1273

What do you think of the following sayings? Have you ever heard or perhaps read them?

---

16 Francis Robinson. *Islam and Muslim History in South Asia*. New Delhi: OUP, 2000.

"Yesterday I was clever, so I wanted to change the world. Today I am wise, so I want to change myself."

"Your task is not to seek love, but merely to seek and find all the barriers within yourself that you have built against it."

"Life is a balance between holding on and letting go."

"What you seek is seeking you."

"It's your road, and yours alone. Others may walk it with you, but no one can walk it for you."

In the English-speaking world, by far the most famous Sufi is Mawlawna Muhammad Jalal al-Din al-Rumi, usually referred to simply as Rumi. Lines from his poetry regularly crop up in the inspirational thoughts industry. He is said to be the best-selling poet in the USA today. I have it on good authority that there are English Rumi societies that meet to read and discuss his poetry without a single Muslim present. Some of his works can even be found in Christian bookshops and among items sold on Christian websites – feel free to check for yourself! The quotations most often used in the West are those that chime with our own outlook; they do not necessarily reflect accurately the real Rumi.

So, who was Rumi? What does he have to do with Islam?

Rumi was born in what is now the border area of Afghanistan and Tajikistan and grew up speaking Persian. His father Baha al-Din was a scholar and teacher of Islam, well versed in both the law and the mystical side of Islam, a preacher and a poet. He was not a follower of any particular shaykh. While Rumi was growing up, Baha al-Din moved westwards with his family, eventually settling in Konya in what is now Turkey. Konya is the city known as Iconium in the book of Acts. The area had been predominantly Christian for centuries but was conquered by Muslim

Turks less than 150 years before the family arrived there. The area still had a substantial Christian population. The Seljuk Turks (who preceded the Ottoman Turks) had made Konya the capital of the territory they controlled and it was a thriving town on the frontiers of the Islamic world.

Persian was the primary language of interaction across Central Asia, and most of Rumi's writing is in that language. He also received a thorough education in Arabic and spent time studying in Damascus. Like his father, he was trained to be a scholar. Even as a young man he was famous for his knowledge and his preaching ability. He was clearly a very gifted individual. He already had a reputation as a teacher of Islamic law and of Sufi disciplines, with many students eager to learn from him, but then he met a man who filled him with fresh inspiration. Shams al-Din, a wandering mystic from Tabriz, was looking for a worthy disciple. There are several accounts of what happened when they met. What they have in common is that Rumi realised that Shams al-Din had a type of knowledge that he had not encountered before. For a few years, they had an intense friendship, and Rumi learned to pursue the knowledge of God in a much more intense and personal way.

Rumi and those around him developed ways of seeking God involving music and movement known as *sama'*, which literally means listening. It is about generating high levels of attentiveness. The object is to lose awareness of self and to be taken up with awareness of God. For Rumi and his disciples, the key to knowing God was to discover his love for his creation and to love him perfectly. The Sufi movement that started with Rumi and his disciples is known as the Mevlevi Tariqa. It was Rumi's son Sultan Walad who gave the movement form, and it spread rapidly through the Islamic world. Its most distinctive feature is the whirling dervish.

He wrote a number of books, the most famous of which is the Mathnavi (also spelled Masnavi), which is regarded today as one of the greatest literary works in the Persian language. It is written entirely as poetry. Like Shakespeare, Rumi took well-known stories and recast them to suit his own purposes. Unlike Shakespeare, his purpose was religious, and so the Mathnavi includes extensive commentary on Qur'anic passages. He was not, however, writing a textbook. Those who approach Rumi with a view to reducing his thought to bullet points soon become frustrated. He never attempted to produce a systematic theology or overriding theory. He did not see it as necessary to eliminate ambiguity as a Western textbook might. For Rumi, truth lay beyond language. He wrote for the general population rather than for scholars, seeking to inspire the people to press deeper and to seek experiential knowledge of God. It seems that he did not believe that a seamless set of propositions and definitions could help anyone in the pursuit of the knowledge of God. He believed that all human beings needed help from a guide more advanced or gifted than themselves. Personal effort and searching would never be enough.

Some have regarded Rumi as a spiritual guide who transcends all religions. One famous verse reads:

Hindus praise me in the terms of India
And the Sindis praise in terms of Sind
I am not made pure by their magnificats
It is they who become pure and precious
We do not look to language or words
We look inside to find intent and rapture.[17]

To read this text as indicating that all religions are the same or of equal worth would be a mistake. It is rather saying that there is only one God, all people seek to worship him and God reads the heart of all.

Certainly, Rumi's teaching was such that he expected to encounter God in all people and saw the whole creation as loved by God. He welcomed Jews and Christians and had friends among them. Since worship was all

---

17 Franklin D. Lewis. *Rumi. Past and Present, East and West.* London: Oneworld, 2000. Revised 2008, page 406.

about love, and God loved all he had made, he found no room for sectarian or confrontational approaches. Many of the lines of his poetry that one hears quoted seem to be expressions of spiritual wisdom that anyone might appreciate. However, he himself was unambiguously Islamic. For Rumi, Muhammad was the height of perfection, and the Qur'an the supreme revelation. Like Jilani, he is reputed to have brought many Jews and Christians into Islam.

He took issue with reading the Qur'an literally and taking the surface meaning as the true meaning. He rejected exposition based on human reasoning. To this extent, he was at odds with some Islamic authorities. For Rumi, only the person who had died to self-centredness and become inflamed by the love of God could really have any perception of the truth, but for him the Qur'an and the person of Muhammad remained the essential lenses everyone needed.

Sufi Celebrities?

THE MAGAZINE *Egypt Today* recently described Shaykh Hamza Yusuf as a kind of theological rock star and likened him to Elvis. How can this be?

We live in a world of global media which seeks celebrities. Sufism is extraordinarily adaptable to circumstances. Today there are many, many Sufi shaykhs, but we are going to focus on those who have attained special international prominence, aided by modern media.

Before we get to Hamza Yusuf, we need to meet some others. In 2006, secular researcher David Damrel described the Sufi movement known as Naqshbandi-Haqqaniya as "one of the fastest growing and most important [Sufi] orders in Western Europe and North America." Though its immediate origins were in the eastern Mediterranean rather than the Indian subcontinent, it was gaining many members from the South Asian communities in Britain.[18]

Damrel was describing one branch of the Naqshbandi Sufi order, a label that takes in a whole range of Sufi networks. The Naqshbandiyya Haqqaniya was founded by Shaykh Nazim Haqqani who had become a sort of Sufi superstar.

---

18 David Damrel, *Aspects Of Naqshbandi-Haqqani Order in North America* in Malik & Hinnels, *Sufism in the West*, (London: Routledge 2006), 115.

Nazim Haqqani was born in the Turkish part of Cyprus in 1922. The story goes that while he was studying chemical engineering in Istanbul he was drawn into the serious study of Islam. He is said to have investigated seven Sufi orders before choosing the Naqshbandiyya-Khalidiya order. He pursued his spiritual exploration in Syria, and eventually took the oath of allegiance to Shaykh Abdullah al-Daghestani in Damascus. Under Daghestani's direction, he travelled and preached extensively within the region. Following the death of Daghestani in 1973, he moved to Lebanon where he established a community and formed an alliance with the influential Kabbani family.

Haqqani started visiting London each year in Ramadan, claiming to have been commanded to do so by his master, Daghestani, and to have been given a mission to the West by Muhammad himself. He later went on to establish what he termed an Islamic Priory in Tottenham in 1992 with funds from the Sultan of Brunei. He sent Shaykh Hisham al-Kabbani as his representative to the USA in 1990, who established a strong and high-profile presence in Haqqani's name.

Haqqani engaged with Westerners, especially New Agers and others seeking enlightenment from the East. The growing interest in Eastern spirituality, starting in the 1960s, had brought Sufism into some European circles, primarily as a form of spirituality rather than as an expression of Islam. Haqqani tapped into this interest, and adapted his message to be inclusive for such seekers. He was able to justify this approach by referring to sayings in the *hadeeth* such as, "Speak in accordance with people's understanding." While being strictly devout in his own practice of Islam, he greeted all seekers with friendly tolerance and never criticised them. He made use of the language of the New Age movement, and accepted invitations to non-Muslim events. In 1999, he visited Glastonbury and set up a Haqqaniya presence there.

It was Haqqani's habit after Ramadan to travel overland through Europe on his way back to Lebanon or Cyprus, stopping in several countries to encourage his followers there. In the 1990s he started visiting the USA as well. He was willing to accept *bay'ah* (allegiance) from would-be followers during his visits, even though there was no prospect of them spending any time with him in the way required in the days of classic Sufism. *Suhba*, spending time in the company of a shaykh, was practised during the time of his visits, and extended first through written materials and then using the internet. Many of the homilies he gave during such visits are now available online, so that followers could practise *suhba* from afar. Similarly, an American-based website even offered online *bay'ah*, the personal oath of allegiance. The *zikir* he taught to followers includes *rabita* (being bound to the shaykh) through an intentional focus on Haqqani as the prime connection with Muhammad and the divine. The *zikir* includes the vocal chanting of the *khatam al-khwajagan* which recounts his own spiritual lineage. While such things were once communicated in seclusion to a would-be spiritual elite, they are now available via the worldwide web.

Haqqani traced his own *silsila*, his spiritual lineage, through the Naqshbandi masters back to Muhammad via Abu Bakr, the first Caliph, as evidenced in the order's publications and websites. In the introduction to a book by Haqqani posthumously published, Hisham Kabbani further asserts that Haqqani's mother's lineage included Rumi, and that his father's genealogy included the great Sufi scholar Abdal-Qadir al-Jilani. For Sufis, lineage is about authority, not history. None of these claims on their own account for his success. The man had charisma; the lineage was published to justify it, to silence critics and to give assurance to followers.

The few Asian Sufi shaykhs who had found themselves living among the immigrant communities in the West during the 1980s and 1990s were mainly preoccupied with preserving the traditional religious culture. Haqqani addressed himself to the wider public, commenting on current affairs and giving advice to the secular authorities. For example, he spoke out during the UK foot and mouth outbreak of 2001, advising vaccination rather than mass slaughter. He commented on the death of Princess Diana, and used it as an opportunity to affirm the values of *shari'a*, saying that if she had lived according to divine law she would not have come to a tragic end. He addressed financial crises by denouncing the whole un-Islamic banking system, and claiming that the root of the problem was paper money, when the divinely approved currency was gold. On all such matters, he spoke with a calm, otherworldly authority, like a messenger from a higher plane.

As a result of his high profile and his success with Westerners, he caught the attention of British Muslims of Pakistani heritage. Here was a man who held his own in Western culture and was not simply a manifestation of the spirituality of their grandparents' village. Haqqani was not the first Naqshbandi shaykh to become active among South Asians in the UK. Shaykhs of Pakistani origin had been active since the early 1960s, but functioned in Urdu and mainly addressed themselves to continuing their own tradition.

The Asians who have responded to Haqqani are mainly British-born. As many commentators have observed, this generation was having to contend not only with living as a minority in a highly secular culture, but also with an English-speaking Islamic fundamentalist movement. Led by the most highly educated, the Salafist movement called for a return to what they see as "true Islam", as opposed to the forms of Asian spirituality that second-generation migrants had been brought up with. The Salafists condemned it as a deviant form of Islam, corrupted by Hinduism. The new generation could see the flaws in their parents' religion, rooted as it was in specific villages in the subcontinent, but they didn't much like the radical alternative.

Haqqani gained a following among such British-born Asians by embodying the cosmology and values of their traditional heritage, while also being located in an international expression of Islam. He addressed the challenges of a secular world from what looked like a position of strength. The fact that he was drawing a following among Westerners could only enhance his credibility.

In addition to general Sufi teaching, Haqqani brought in an apocalyptic dimension. He regularly spoke of the imminent arrival of the *Mahdi* and the *Dajjal* (Anti-Christ), both precursors to the coming of Christ in Islamic end-time scenarios. He asserted that the *Mahdi* was already on Earth awaiting his moment to emerge, and that he, Haqqani, was in communication with him. As many a cult leader has found in the past, speaking in such a way adds urgency to a call to engage. And like cult leaders of old, he gave some specific predictions which failed to materialise. For example, amid the anxieties attending the approach of the year 2000, he predicted a range of catastrophes which did not happen. His movement lost some momentum at that point.

Haqqani succeeded in scaling up a Sufi order to become a global force. As Haqqani aged, his deputies, the Lebanese brothers Hisham and Adnan Kabbani, took an increasing share of the work. Hisham led the movement in the USA, where considerable amounts of literature were produced. He was responsible for publishing an English language encyclopaedia of Islam which was both scholarly and Sufi-oriented, in order to counteract the prevailing narrative claiming that the only true Islam was that of the fundamentalists.

When Haqqani died in 2014, his son Mehmet succeeded as head of the order, and inherited a substantial international network. I have met him twice, and he does not seem to have the charisma of his father, but he travels extensively, receives visitors in Cyprus from all over the world, and regularly puts out nuggets of spiritual wisdom via social media.

WESTERN CONVERT SUFIS

In the mid-1990s, three Sufi figures emerged on the UK scene who were new in several respects. All three had engaged in serious Islamic study abroad. One was Hamza Yusuf (born Mark Hanson). He was a white American from California who became a Muslim in 1977. The other two were fellow American Nuh Ha Mim Keller and Abdal Hakim Murad (born

Tim Winter), who was British. They connected with the rising generation of British Asian Muslims through magazines and conferences, and continue to do so through the internet. Increasingly, young Asians have been associated with their initiatives. These men did not set up their own chain of mosques; rather their influence energised Sufi-minded people within existing mosques and associations.

While Keller and Murad became self-effacing but highly influential academics, Yusuf thrived in the spotlight of publicity. Charismatic, telegenic and engaging, he had been mentored by Abdalqadir as-Sufi – a Scot, born Ian Dallas – who had embraced Islam in 1967 and was attached to a Sufi order based in Morocco. As-Sufi had established a small, tight-knit, exclusive community in Norwich, UK, made up of highly educated British and American converts to Islam.[19] He had kept his followers away from traditional Asian Sufis, but wrote extensively for the general Muslim population, and translated Sufi texts into English, promoting radical Sufism as a cure for the ills of the West. Yusuf moved to Norwich to learn from As-Sufi.

After a while, Yusuf moved on, and pursued further studies in UAE, Algeria and Mauritania. Along with another American convert he founded the Zaytun Institute in California, a college that emphasised traditional Islamic disciplines. It became the first Islamic college in the USA to attain academic respectability.

As a preacher, he is often described as a firebrand. His readiness to accept speaking invitations and TV interviews has given him a huge following. His preaching and teaching are disseminated via YouTube, Twitter and Instagram, and I find Muslims living in the old industrial towns of England quoting him. The magazine *Egypt Today* quoted at the top of this chapter dubbed him "the Elvis Presley of western Muslims".

---

19   Yasin Dutton. *The Da'wa of Shaykh Abdalqadir as-Sufi* in *Sufism in Britain*, editors Geaves & Gabriel. London: Bloomsbury, 2014.

Yusuf preaches in English, but particularly emphasises the priority of studying Arabic. He has translated some famous devotional and doctrinal works from Arabic into English. For Asian Muslims living in an Urdu-dominated subculture, this was a lifeline: English language materials drawn directly from Arabic sources, accessible, credible (in Islamic terms) and reflecting the richness of the mystical traditions.

In marked contrast to the views promoted by the political Islamic groups influential in universities in the 1990s, Yusuf and the other new Western shaykhs affirmed the values of classical Islam. Secular researcher Sadek Hamid identified seven key themes in their writing and speaking, which included classical Islamic theology and social engagement. The commitment to social engagement set them apart from the Pakistani Sufi leaders, but was something they had in common with Haqqani.

Unlike any of the previous movements, they combined Western voices with Arabic scholarship (rather than Urdu). Neither their route into Islam nor their scholarship owed anything at all to the Asian Sufi presence in the UK, but in Hamid's words, "The combined output effect of these three figures altered the terms of reference in activist circles and introduced a whole new discourse into issues that until then had not been addressed by existing Islamist organisations. In effect, they had re-established Sufism as a legitimate and necessary part of mainstream Islam."[20]

LIVERPOOL, THE GATEWAY FOR YEMEN

A less well known but highly significant figure in the repositioning of Sufism in the UK is Ibrahim Osi-Efa. Born in Liverpool of Nigerian parents, Osi-Efa became an activist on race issues in the early 1980s in his teens. Through learning about Malcolm X, he was drawn to rediscovering Islam. Initially he

---

20   Sadek Hamid. *The Rise of the Traditional Islam Network(s). Neo-Sufism and British Muslim Youth*, in *Sufism in Britain*, Eds Geaves and Gabriel (London: Bloomsbury, 2015), 182.

was drawn towards the fundamentalist groups, but was dissatisfied with their lack of depth. In 1992 he started a holistic education programme in Liverpool for young people, which taught Islam, Arabic, health and martial arts. It continues today under the name the Greensville Trust. Sensing his own need to go deeper, he embarked on the study of Arabic. In the early 1990s, he met Yusuf Hamza and invited him to teach in Liverpool for a month. It was Osi-Efa who invited Yusuf to address a major European conference in August 1995 which brought him to prominence in the UK. Osi-Efa went on to study in Mauritania and Yemen and joined the Ba'Alawi Sufi order.

Following the 1995 conference, Osi-Efa discussed with others how they might establish accessible Islamic study programmes. Out of this came the "Micro Madrasa", modelled through the Greensville Trust in Liverpool, with study sessions at three levels: the Light Study, a one-day introductory programme; the *Deen* Intensive, a full weekend; and the *Rihla*, a one-month summer school. In addition, and in partnership with visiting Yemeni shaykhs, Osi-Efa now runs residential retreats in Wales each summer called The Trodden Path. All these give lay people access to the traditional Islamic sciences. Graduates of his programme go on to set up their own local "para-mosque" bodies, running classes and charitable activities.

One important distinctive of Osi-Efa's contribution to Sufism in the UK is the high value he sets on Islamic sports. While some mosques, in response to youth culture, do run football or table tennis, the Greensville Trust argues from Islamic sources that there are four truly Islamic sports, namely wrestling, archery, horse riding and swimming. These are promoted theologically as valuable spiritual exercises, an important part of mastering the lower self, a major theme in Sufi Islam. As the twenty-first century unfolds, Islamic sports are becoming more common around the country (as an online search will show), meeting the needs of young people for such activities and promoting practical *ihsan*.

Osi-Efa is not really an A-list celebrity in that he mainly operates below the radar. He is a man of great energy and influence, but he is also the

UK representative for a group of Yemeni shaykhs headed by Habib Umar Bin Hafiz. Umar has never been to the UK but has many *mureeds* here, thanks to the efforts of Osi-Efa. Umar is something of a media celebrity. I am finding people from a whole range of traditions featuring him on their Facebook pages. He and his associates from Yemen, all of whom claim to be direct descendants of Muhammad and who all go by the title *Habib*, come from a valley in Yemen where Sufi Islam has been practised for centuries in relative isolation. It has the appeal of apparently being unspoiled, rooted in a purer past. It was always a place that seekers go to, not that people come from. Today Umar and his travelling representatives are becoming known all over the world, through social media, as models of devotional piety: socially conservative, but gentle, warm and inclusive.

THE SWEDISH-SPEAKING SYRIAN

Finally, we come to Shaykh Muhammad Abu l-Huda al-Yaqoubi. He is from Syria and is currently living in exile in Morocco. He is on record as opposing both President Assad and the so-called Islamic State. Yaqoubi comes from a family of famous Syrian scholars who have held many prestigious positions in Syria. His Islamic academic credentials are impeccable and he is fluent in Arabic, English and Swedish. He travels widely, speaking at conferences held at universities and other major venues, which are then live-streamed to the general public. He has a reputation for rigour. One of his British *mureeds* told me how he had gone to a conference and found Yaqoubi to be the principal speaker. He was so impressed that he and his mates asked for an audience with the shaykh to pledge their allegiance. The shaykh spoke to them briefly and then told them they were not ready and sent them away. It was a couple of heart-searching years later when my friend was accepted as a *mureed*.

Yaqoubi impresses as one who truly knows his stuff. His followers see him as the model of true Islam, a descendant of Muhammad who embodies him in the present. He teaches in a clear straightforward way about how Muslims should live in a secular world. He advocates classic

Sufi disciplines, including *zikir*, requiring the 100-fold repetition of certain Arabic phrases.

The shaykh, though from the Arab world, addresses himself to English-speaking Muslims of Pakistani heritage among whom he is building a following. He was quoted in a World of Sufis tweet (29-09-2016) as saying: "The problem is people blame black magic for every difficulty that they face. This is wrong. Psychological disorders, illusions or real failures in life are more commonly the causes, not black magic. From the aspect of culture, the Indian subcontinent is affected a lot. One of the main reasons is loss of confidence in Allah." Here he distances himself from the standard fear of the invisible world while affirming a radical focus on God himself.

This shaykh has broken new ground by founding the Women's Muslim College in the UK, which runs classes in Birmingham, Leicester, Hounslow and, inevitably these days, via the internet. The principal of the college is Glasgow-born British Asian woman Shaykha Safia Shahid, who we shall meet in the next chapter. This is not one of those institutions to which Muslims send their women to keep them domesticated; it is all about meeting the world head on.

Women in Sufism

You MIGHT BE WONDERING IF SUFISM is an exclusively male preserve. After all, the parts of the world where Sufism has developed are deeply patriarchal, and Islam has a reputation for relegating women to the sidelines. So far, this book has not made any mention of women. But then, Sufism does have a knack of subverting our expectations.

Back in chapter 3, we talked about the circles of Sufism. In the outer circle whole communities acknowledge Sufism as a real and legitimate thing, and interact with it accordingly. That widest circle certainly includes many, many women. Around the world, they are often present in large numbers as pilgrims visiting the Sufi masters and saints, both living and dead. In the October 2010 edition of the online St Francis Magazine, Sophia Kim writes eloquently of the place of Sufi sites in the lives of ordinary women in Asia.

> Once a woman shared [with me] the hardships of her life. Her husband had lost his job two years previously, and since then she had been visiting the shrine whenever she had a day off. For her, the shrine was a place to recharge and renew herself so that she could endure the hardships of life. Many women save money to travel to the famous shrines that are often a long way from where they live. They want to get comfort to face insecure futures. The shrines become a place of release from all the difficulties of life, a place of taking rest and receiving comfort beside the tomb of their beloved saint.

These scenarios are repeated over and over across the Muslim world. Sufi saints, whether dead or alive, are seen as intermediaries with the world of unseen powers, and ultimately with God who decides the fate of all. We find that alongside the belief that everything is determined by the absolute sovereignty of the Almighty, there is also a great fascination with figures who may have enough influence to change fate. What people in these settings are most certain of is their own powerlessness. This is perhaps most keenly felt by women, as they grapple with the incessant demands and burdens of domestic life. The belief and the hope that benign, accessible powers are there for them runs strongly through their lives and is modelled to their children.

If many women are believers in Sufi Islam and engage with it as petitioners of Sufi saints, can also they be accepted as devoted disciples on the Sufi path?

MODERN MUREEDAS

I was attending a community event hosted by the central mosque in a small town in northern England. I found myself talking to a young woman who turned out to be a primary school teacher. I asked her if this was the mosque where she normally worshipped. No, she said, normally she went to the Minhaj-ul-Quran mosque. Now, I knew two things about the Minhaj-ul-Quran (MQ) movement, namely that it sought to combine Sufi values with a modern organisational structure under Shaykh Tahir-ul-Qadri, and that every branch had an active women's department. I asked her if she had ever met the shaykh. She was surprised that I knew so much about it and replied in the affirmative. I asked if she was a *mureeda* (a female *mureed*). Yes, she said, but she was a follower of Pir Siddiqui. Both Pir Siddiqui and Shaykh ul-Qadri are thoroughly rooted in Pakistan, and virtually all their followers are Asian, whichever country they might live in. They both want to see traditional Sufi spirituality brought into the modern world. They set a high value on secular education alongside religious education. Both advocate a place for women in the public sphere, and find themselves at odds with many more traditional scholars in Pakistan.

When Shaykh Nazim launched his mission to the West, he frequented New Age type events and welcomed both men and women as *mureeds*. When he met with his Western followers, the meetings were unsegregated. In other settings, he followed a more traditional pattern, but he still accepted female followers. He operated an extreme open-door policy compared with most of his peers, demanding very little of his followers, and the effect was to build up a very mixed following, which in turn drew in others looking for an alternative lifestyle.

Dr Julianne Hazen is an American academic who has done some research on Westerners converting to Islam through Sufism. She herself is a *mureeda* following a shaykh from the Balkans who settled in the USA and who is both a scientist and a teacher of Sufism.

So yes, women do become disciples and follow the Sufi path, at least in some places and in some settings. Up to this point, we have made no mention of female shaykhs or saints. Do they exist?

THE SHAYKHA FROM GLASGOW

Yes, they do. You can easily find Shaykha Safia Shahid online. She has emerged under the umbrella of Shaykh Yaqoubi of the Shadhili tradition. She is principal of the Women's Muslim College which runs classes in several UK cities and online. She is a scholar in her own right and an active Sufi. A SufiWorld tweet in 2017 posted an image of her, declaring: "The door of sainthood is open to women, not just men. It can be acquired by a wife yet not by her husband; she can attain gifts from God while he does not."

Shaykha Safia was born and raised in Glasgow, Scotland, and has studied in the Middle East. Among other things, she runs retreats for

Muslim women in the UK. Could her dramatic declaration be a case of welding a modern Western agenda onto an ancient Islamic tradition?

THE LEGENDARY RABI'A

Nothing is ever quite that simple. One of the most famous early Sufis was Rabi'a al-Adawiya, a woman who lived in the city of Basra, southern Iraq, and is believed to have died in the year 801. She was famous for her rejection of the world and utter commitment to God expressed through devotional poetry. She is best known for the verse that runs:

> O Lord, if I worship You because of Fear of Hell, then burn me in Hell;
> If I worship You because I desire Paradise, then exclude me from Paradise;
> But if I worship You for Yourself alone, then deny me not your Eternal Beauty.

She wrote no books, and what we know of her has come down mixed with legend, but she is highly regarded in the Sufi tradition and thought of as a saint. However, she stands out as *the* female Sufi saint, often the only one that people have heard of. If we dig deeper, we can find records of women of great piety and charisma, but they generally have not occupied the public space and have not taken disciples. It is true to say that men have been much more prominent through the centuries, but Shaykha Safia does have precedents to draw on. Those that are better-known are usually closely connected with prominent men, and that accounts for what prominence they attained.

However, it is a simple fact that much of what has gone on in the past and goes on now is not well documented. I was reading just recently of an anthropologist writing about Uzbekistan in Central Asia. He described how female *pirs* using Sufi formulas acted as mediums, accessing departed saints on behalf of petitioners. The researcher was actually writing about how the assumptions that shaped the work of researchers led to them not seeing what was actually there. I have also recently seen an all-female *zikir* circle on YouTube which is a long-standing tradition in Chechnya.

MAMA SHAYKHAS

Anthropologist Dr Pnina Werbner has written extensively on the transplantation of Sufism into the UK within the Asian community. She describes a woman in Manchester of Pakistani origin called Baji Saeeda Khatoon who was the head of the Azimiyya Sufi grouping in Europe until her death in 2010. She is said to have been able to see the invisible world since she was a small child. Her following included both men and women. She travelled regularly to other cities in the UK to meet them. Werbner observed some of her gatherings, which generally numbered 15–25 people at a time, and described her leading *zikir* sessions, giving lectures and exercising a motherly role to a warm and friendly group. The followers came from a variety of backgrounds, and their association with the shaykha was like a second family to them. Werbner interviewed some of the followers, who saw nothing surprising about having a female shaykh.[21] Baji Saeeda was not a major figure on the world stage, but she is indicative of the variety which is a feature of Sufi-rich environments. Since reading about her, I myself have come across some men who followed her.

Sufism is highly adaptive. We now live a world in which Islam is regularly given a hard time over the status of women. We also have a new generation of Muslim women who are educated and engaging with their religion, making their own choices. At the present time, there is a growing body of research conducted by Muslim women and by secular academics which demonstrates the presence of female mystics in Islam through the centuries. Sufism offers a whole range of possibilities that the claustrophobic world of Islamic law does not. The new generation Sufi movements is already making ways for women to participate, and we can expect to see the emergence of many more female Sufi leaders.

---

21 Pnina Werbner. *Sufi Cults, Intimate Relations and National Pakistani Networking in Britain.* In Jamal Malik (ed) *Muslims in Europe Munster*: Lit Verlag, 2004.

Darkness

I WAS SPEAKING WITH A CHRISTIAN ANTHROPOLOGIST who had been conducting research into Sufism in a Muslim-majority country. These days the discipline of anthropology does not allow researchers to observe a practice as an outsider and then draw your own conclusions; no, you have to get right inside the world of the people you are studying and be ready to distinguish between your own feelings and prejudices and the experience of the people you are studying. Consequently, his research required him to join in as a temporary follower of a Sufi shaykh, with the shaykh's permission, of course, and to participate in all the activities of the *tariqa*. Pleased to find someone who had some idea of the things he was talking about, he spoke to me with enthusiasm. Then I asked a question. "Were you aware of any spiritual darkness?" His face changed. "Absolutely. It was oppressive. It was *so* dark."

Readers may have noticed that up to this point I have said very little that might be termed uncomplimentary about Islam or about Sufism. Some readers may well have been troubled by my readiness to talk about Sufis seeking close knowledge of God or living in the love of God. Surely, I should be saying "seeking proximity to Allah"? And in all probability such readers will have given up reading this book long before they reached this point.

There is only one God. His name in Arabic is Allah. Christians and others had used that name before the rise of Islam. Muhammad's message to Christians and Jews was about the God they worshipped. There are not two beings, one called God and one called Allah. And that is the point. Islam never set out to proclaim a new deity. If it had, things might have been easier for us. It fashioned a new narrative about the one we already knew.

That narrative systematically steers people away from what God says of himself in the Bible, how he has revealed himself in Christ, and his eternal plan to bring salvation to humankind. It repudiates his coming in Christ. It denies the cross and the resurrection. The whole plan of salvation is set aside. Biblical characters are recast in new roles in a spiritual history which denies historic truth and supports a different vision of God. Same God, different story about him. That is the nub of the matter.

The alert reader may notice that I never describe Muhammad as a prophet. Whether he started as a sincere seeker and was led astray or was a false prophet from the start, I don't pretend to know. The very best forms of Sufism, with all their fine words, noble ideals and preoccupation with divine love, are always channelled through and shaped by the person of Muhammad. One might argue that some Sufi teachers have subverted the darker aspects of Islam and moved it in a more wholesome direction, but these are only shades of grey. If we believe that the most important act of God since his creation of the world is his redemption of humanity through Christ, if that is the central focus of all the purposes of God, then anyone who claims to speak for God without acknowledging this truth is against him and not for him.

Why, some will ask, was this not my starting point? I have two reasons. The first is that if we want to engage with people – real flesh and blood people who live in our neighbourhoods – we need to appreciate how they see themselves. Our knowing *why they are not Christian* is not the same as knowing *who they think they are*. The second reason is that an approach controlled by the need to prove how dark someone's faith is leads to us being unable to relate to them as people. It engenders fear. It validates distance. Instead of meeting them as real, complicated people, they become cardboard cut-outs representing a sinister "something else". Jesus never treated anyone in that way.

With such as an approach it is unlikely that we will form an accurate picture of them or their lives. We end up building a case against them, selecting the evidence that suits our agenda, whether it is fair or not. We form a picture that satisfies our prejudices and increases our sense of self-righteousness. Actually, we benefit from having our complacency rattled from time to time. We do ourselves no favours when we populate our world with simplistic stereotypes.

One might also add that when we think we know about people simply because we have been told how wrong they are, we find ourselves utterly wrong-footed when they turn out to be gracious and spiritually minded. We need to have some idea of how they perceive themselves. They believe they are the good guys. It is important that we have some notion of how it is that they set such high value on something which is not from God.

There is something distasteful about describing someone as sinister simply because their beliefs are incorrect. We use the term "darkness" to refer to mere ignorance, the absence of truth, but we also use the term to refer to something more actively negative, a power that works against what is true and right. For me and for my anthropologist friend to claim that Sufism is dark, we should offer some evidence.

IDOLATRY AND THE OCCULT

When Muslims hear us worshipping Jesus, they call us idolaters. We agree with them that worshipping anyone other than God is wrong, but we disagree that worshipping Jesus is idolatry because Jesus is divine. The whole Bible, Old and New Testaments, regards idolatry as a doorway to every kind of evil. Meanwhile Muslims deny that they worship Muhammad. Sufis compose hymns of praise to him and call upon him to be with them. They affirm that he is a created being, and they claim they are not worshipping him as a god, yet they address prayers to him. They address him as a living and present individual. That sounds like worship to most of us. We can see parallels in Christian tradition with the veneration of saints and the conflicting views about that. One tradition's veneration of Mary is, in another tradition's view, blatant idolatry.

Coming back to Sufi Muslims, we would not be the only ones who would lump their behaviour into the category of idolatry. The more conventional Muslims make the same judgement. Twice a year, our local Salafi mosque, following a Saudi-style interpretation of Islam, holds prayers in the park. Each time, the *imam*, flanked by powerful loudspeakers, projecting his voice into the neighbourhood, states that it is totally contrary to true religion to address any praise or prayer to any being other than God himself. He is not having a go at Christians. He is addressing his Sufi-minded neighbours.

In the Old Testament, in Deuteronomy 18:9–14, the people were warned against anyone practising divination – seeking knowledge of the unseen – communicating with the dead and accessing unseen spiritual powers. Sufi practitioners do all of these things to one degree or another. In many parts of the world, they have displaced shamans and witchdoctors by taking over their business and combining Islam with delivering remedies. One of the foundational ideas of Sufism is that when an individual attains closeness to God, he gains power over nature and is able to deal with invisible powers.

While Westerners raised with a secular view of the world relegate the idea of invisible powers to mere folk beliefs and superstitions, orthodox Islam requires a belief in such powers. Regular, text-based Islam insists that the world is inhabited by an invisible race of beings called the *jinn* who live side by side with us. They may be good, they may be bad, but they are always powerful. They are invisible powers. Muhammad addressed them in the Qur'an. They are not an optional extra. Christians who have retained a Biblical world view also acknowledge the presence of invisible powers, but are taught not to trust any of them or to seek them out. Christ is supreme over them, and it is to him that we address ourselves. Sufi practitioners, on the other hand, are expected to draw on them. Sufi saints are said to possess *baraka*, loosely translated "blessing", meaning an impersonal, invisible, benign force. It is the desire to be touched by *baraka* that draws millions to the great Sufi shrines of the East, not a desire to express an appreciation for the shaykh's insights.

Earlier I mentioned a man I know who continues to commune with his shaykh years after the shaykh died.[22] He lives in my neighbourhood and works in a local school. Sitting in his living room, seeing the portrait of the shaykh, and hearing him describe his experiences was one of the spookiest I have ever known. I could see it in his eyes. I could feel it in the room. This was a man who lived in the presence of an invisible power.

A number of times I have sat in on Sufi chanting sessions. Some were basically private; others were intended to be public. They all have the same feel. I would not encourage anyone else to attend any of them. In the public ones, people were encouraged to relax, and to let the spiritual words touch their souls, whether they joined in or not. The chanting was in Arabic, and I know enough Arabic to understand the words, but no translation was ever offered to the public. Once it got going it was hypnotic, carrying people along. "No need to understand, just let it in." It felt extremely dark.

---

22   For example, Romans 8:38–39; Ephesians 1:18–23.

Mysteries

"**APPARENTLY THE MUSLIMS IN THAT MOSQUE** are not proper Muslims. They worship Muhammad as some mystical light from before creation," my Christian friend said, as he showed me round town. He was talking about the biggest and most high-profile mosque in an English town that also had several other mosques.

Probably the thing we Christians are most surprised about when we delve into Islamic Sufism is the *Noor Muhammadi* teaching. It is indeed the notion that Muhammad existed before creation as divinely created light through whom and for whom the world was made. If that expression seems to have a biblical ring about it, there is a good reason; it may be because it sounds suspiciously like John 1:3, 1 Corinthians 8:6 and Colossians 1:16, among others.

The idea is that before God created anything else, he created from his own glory a heavenly light. That light is present in some form in all that he subsequently made. It is particularly present in the prophets, but it is present in everyone. Eventually, in the fullness of time, that light became flesh and dwelt among us, living as the perfect messenger and indeed the perfect man, casting no shadow. Furthermore, although his body died, Muhammad continues to be present and aware, accessible to those who are enlightened.

What I have described represents the fullest form of the *Noor Muhammadi* (Muhammadan Light) teaching. For the Barelvi movement of the Indian subcontinent, it is one of their defining beliefs. About 36% of the mosques in the UK are Barelvi-led, so this is not an obscure, peripheral sect. Although many UK mosques are led by "reformers" of one kind or another, Barelvi beliefs may well be held by those who attend those mosques too, because for many communities in Pakistan, India and Bangladesh, this is the orthodoxy.

SO WHERE DID *THAT* COME FROM?

This prompts some questions. Are we talking about some kind of Indianisation of Islam? Perhaps a crossover from Hinduism/Buddhism? Is it a teaching that only emerged relatively late in the day, an elaboration built up on the foundation of simple Islam which has been allowed to accumulate over the centuries? Is there any basis for these ideas in the Qur'an? One might also be tempted to ask the politically incorrect question of whether these teachings are only held by those not yet blessed by an education in science and reason.

Sidi Muhammad Ibn al-Habib, (1876-1972) wrote these words in a devotional poem.

> Muhammad is the fountain-head of lights and darknesses [sic] and the source of their emergence from the presence of pre-endless-time. So his light was the first of lights… From him all things were clothed in their origination in existence, and their continuity is uninterruptedly from him. The prophets and messengers have come from him one by one, and all the kings and all the creatures.[23]

Sidi Muhammad was a Sufi master who lived in Morocco. His brand of spirituality has nothing to do with India. What is more, I originally came

---

23   http://www.wynnechambers.co.uk/pdf/Mawlid.pdf

across this verse on the website of a British lawyer who goes by the name of Ahmad Thompson, a highly educated and very English Muslim.

The great Sufi teacher Abdal-Qadir al-Jilani who was based in Baghdad, the very centre of the Muslim world of his time, penned these words: "Allah Most High first created, from the divine light of His own beauty, the light of Muhammad... This is declared by our master the messenger of Allah in his words, 'Allah first created my soul. He first created it as a divine light.'"[24]

He based this claim on "Muhammad's words", by which he means a *hadeeth*, a saying passed on orally for generations before being written down in a collection. The fact that this was taught in Baghdad in the twelfth century shows that it was current at that time. The fact that he supported the assertion with reference to a text suggests it was not universally agreed upon. The *hadeeth* in question was probably Hadeeth Jabir,[25] which some scholars accept as authentic and others do not. It relates how a companion of Muhammad asked him about creation, and Muhammad obliged him by making this extraordinary claim. For those who believe the account to be authentic, this places the declaration in Muhammad's lifetime, and so for them any thought of it being a later polishing up of the man Muhammad is invalidated.

FURTHER BACK STILL

We might ask how far back we have to go to find this teaching in written form. If we ask this question, we need to bear in mind that even once written records became common in the Muslim world, the oral transmission of teaching was still the preferred means. Books were

---

24 AbdulQadir al-Jilani, *Secret of Secrets* Translated by Tosun Bayrak al-Halvati, (Cambridge: Islamic Texts Society, 1992), 5.

25 al-Qastalani, *Light of the Prophet*, translated by As-Sunna Foundation of America, (http://rasulallah.info/id36.html), 2

reminders of what was orally transmitted, and the authority was in the person rather than in the page.

Two centuries before Jilani, we find al-Hallaj, a famous Sufi, declaring of Muhammad:

> He is and was, and was known before created things and existences and beings. He was and still is remembered before 'before' and after 'after', and before substances and qualities. His substance is completely light,…[26]

In the interest of balance, it should be made known that Hallaj was executed for heresy, but the heresy he was executed for was not in relation to Muhammad. Al-Hallaj claimed to be so caught up in God that he could say "I am the Truth." And so they killed him.

The Qur'an is not a narrative text and does not provide a biography of Muhammad. The first biographies we know of (known as the *seera* literature) were written a good hundred years after his death, and the earliest documents still available to us were written closer to two hundred years after his death. The main early Sunni *seeras* make reference to some supernatural qualities in Muhammad, but none of them describe him as the first of creation.

However, that does not prove that the teaching was not already present. The early centuries of Islam were wracked with conflicts. One of the elements that ran through those conflicts concerned the question of political authority. Should leadership remain in the hands of Muhammad's family or should leaders be appointed by the community? This is the origin of the Sunni/Shi'a split. That writers benefitting from the patronage of Sunni rulers did not draw on traditions about Muhammad's special place

26 Al-Hallaj, Mansur, *The Tawasin*, Translated by Aisha AbdarRahman At-Tarjumana, (http://www.hermetics.org/pdf/Tawasin.pdf), 2.

in creation is not surprising. It would imply that his biological descendants might also have a special status, which is the Shi'ite position. One of the *seera* writers was Mas'udi (895–945). He was a Shi'ite and wrote:

> God, when he intended to establish the laws of the universe, to lay the seed of generation, and to produce the creation, gave to it first the form of fine dust before he formed the earth, and raised the heavens. He dwelt in his unapproachable glory, and in the unity of his power. Then he put down a particle of his light, and made lighten a sparkle of his splendour. The dust rose, and the light was concentrated in the centre of this floating dust. This represented the figure of our prophet MOHAMMED, on whom may rest the blessing of God![27]

THE LIGHT OF MUHAMMAD IN THE QUR'AN

All that said, no doctrine can have real currency in the Muslim world without some basis in the Qur'an. The text that the teachers of *Noor Muhammadi* tend to go to are Q 5:15: "O People of the Book! Our Messenger has come to you, clarifying for you much of what you kept hidden of the Book, and overlooking much. A light from God has come to you, and a clear Book."[28]

Not unreasonably, it is said that the book is the Qur'an and the light is Muhammad. Q 24:35 waxes lyrical about God being the light and then makes reference to a lamp. The commentators (and traditionally no one expected to understand the Qur'an *without* reference to commentators – it is a mysterious and poetic book) identify the lamp with the person of Muhammad. Similarly, in Q 33:45–46, Muhammad is told he is "an illuminating beacon". This may sound like a far cry from a light that pre-dates creation, but commentators,

---

27 Al-Mas'udi, *Meadows of Gold and Mines of Gems, Volume 1* trans Aloys Sprenger (London: Parbury, Allen, & Co., 1841) digital archive, 51.

28 English renderings of the Qur'an are taken from the ClearQuran (Itani) translation unless otherwise stated.

quoting accounts claiming that Muhammad expanded further on these utterances when questioned by his companions, have plenty of material to work with. The idea of Muhammad's pre-existence is supported by reference to different texts that do not refer to light.

It was some time before formal Qur'anic commentaries began to be written. Tustari (818–896) was one of the early commentators. With reference to the obscure Q 7:172 he wrote:

> For when God, Exalted is He, wanted to create Muhammad He made appear a light from His light, and when it reached the veil of divine majesty it prostrated before God, and from that prostration God created an immense crystal-like column of light, that was inwardly and outwardly translucent, and within it was the essence of Muhammad. Then it stood in service before the Lord of the Worlds for a million years with the essential characteristics of faith, which are the visual beholding of faith, the unveiling of certainty and the witnessing of the Lord. Thus He honoured him with this witnessing, a million years before beginning the creation.[29]

The text is available to us in English through work done by English Muslim academics who value these documents. Shaykh Nuh Keller, the American convert to Islam mentioned earlier, is a highly accomplished scholar, and he supports the teaching.[30]

IS IT A SECRET?

Suffice it to say that the Sufi belief in Muhammad as the first of creation is not held by all Muslims, but it is found right across the Muslim world. It is a view upheld and taught by serious scholars of a variety of backgrounds alive today.

---

29 *Tafsir al-Tustari*, translated A&A Keeler, (Louisville, Fons Vitae, 2011) 76

30 Nuh Ha Mim Keller, *Haqiqa Muhammadiya* Masud.co.uk 1995.

Why then does it not appear in books about Islam written in English? I think the reason is partly that the Western prejudice is to regard the least supernatural version of Islam as the most authentic. It is also, in part, because the streams of Islam most easily available to the West are the law-based reformers who also mistrust the esoteric elements. In addition, the transmission and celebration of these doctrines has been primarily through poetry, song and other devotional material. Westerners tend to regard these as secondary sources when trying to make sense of Islam. The other side of the coin is that, while formal written treatises are written in Arabic for scholars, the devotional materials produced by Sufis and given highly memorable form are often disseminated in local languages and instilled in children at their mother's knee. The popular forms are much more pervasive than the formal texts that we are taught represent the real Islam.

There is perhaps one more thing that should be said. In Q 18:110, God is recorded as telling Muhammad:

> Say, "I am only a human being like you, being inspired that your god is
> One God. Whoever hopes to meet his Lord, let him work righteousness,
> and never associate anyone with the worship of his Lord."

This does seem to be a flat contradiction of the idea that Muhammad was so much more than an ordinary person who happened to have been chosen for a purpose. This text is, of course, used by those Muslims opposed to Sufi teachings, and Sufi leaders have well-rehearsed arguments dealing with the text. I have in my possession a tract written by Tahir-ul-Qadri explaining why *Noor Muhammadi* is still true despite what that verse seems to say.

Nevertheless, there is clearly a case for suspecting that if it were possible to call up Muhammad and consult him about the Muhammadan Light doctrine that he would repudiate it. However, it is not our business to decide what Muslims ought to believe, or to arrange them in some kind of hierarchy of correctness. We need to deal with the people we meet and understand them as they are, and point them to Christ, the Light of the world, through whom and for whom all things were made.

Muhammad and Friends

IT WAS AN IMPRESSIVE SIGHT. A crowd of five thousand men surging down the narrow, terraced streets, squeezing past the parked vehicles on a Sunday morning. I say surged, but it was quite orderly, if rather loud. It took about fifteen minutes for the whole procession to pass. In the lead was a car with speakers mounted on it, belting out devotional songs in Urdu. Leaders carried flags and banners. This was an annual event, the celebration Eid al-Mawlid, that is, the birth of Muhammad. Because the year in the Islamic calendar is 11 days shorter than the standard calendar, the event moves through the seasons.

This march is called a *juloos* (also spelled *jaloos, julus* etc.), and it means a procession. To say that it commemorates the occasion of Muhammad's birth would be misleading. The theme is that Muhammad is "a mercy to all mankind". It is a celebration of his presence, not just his history. It is a practice promoted by Sufis but denounced by reformers. Many a pamphlet has been written and YouTube message circulated to either defend or attack it. Holding a *juloos* on Muhammad's birthday was introduced into the UK in 1973 by Sufi Abdullah, the official representative of Shaykh Zindapir in Pakistan. When Sufi Abdullah proposed holding a *juloos* in Birmingham, local Muslim leaders opposed the idea as something that was simply asking for trouble, but he went ahead.

Anthropologist Dr Pnina Werbner studied Zindapir's movement and documented the introduction of the *juloos* into the UK. She described it in a chapter entitled "Stamping the Earth with the Name of Allah: Julus, Zikir and the Sacralising of Space".[31] Her assessment was that the procession was part of a process of rooting Islam into a locality, making the place more Islamic. As a secular academic, she showed no awareness of prayer walking, but what she was struggling to describe is something that prayer walkers might recognise. Today the *juloos* is performed annually in at least eight locations in the UK.

ISLAMIC SAINTS

Muhammad is seen as a conduit of mercy to the world. Sufi masters are seen as tapping into that presence and giving others access to it. At this point we need to introduce some more technical terms. Several times, we have used the word "saint". This a rough translation of the Arabic word *wali* for which the plural is *awliya*. Spellings in English will vary! A *wali Allah* is a friend of God. Ordinary Muslims would never dare to take such a title for themselves. It is used to refer to people who become especially holy, leaving behind mundane preoccupations and live in communion with God via Muhammad. They are able to mediate with God on behalf of others. Such people are connected to each other in the invisible world across time. All the prophets of the past are regarded as being *awliya*, but the term is mainly used of persons coming after Muhammad, and the term is most often applied to people after they have died.

Of course, in Islam no one can be called a prophet after the time of Muhammad. Muhammad's designation as "the Final Prophet" makes that impossible. The *awliya* are in many respects like prophets, but it would be scandalous to apply that label. One of the thumbnail definitions of Sufis is "people who believe in the *awliya*". Underlying any particular belief about a specific historical individual is a belief that God has organised creation such that the *awliya* should be available to the faithful.

---

31 Pnina Werbner. *Pilgrims of Love: The Anthropology of a Global Sufi Cult*. London C. Hurst & Co, 2004

Shaykh Hisham Kabbani put it this way:

> ...although there are no longer prophets on earth, the Most Merciful Lord has not left His servants without inspired teachers and guides. *Awliya*, holy souls or saints, are the Inheritors of the prophets. Up to the Last Day, these "friends of God", beacons of truth, righteousness and the highest spirituality, will continue in the footsteps of the prophets calling people to their Lord and guiding seekers to His glorious divine Presence.[32]

So, no to prophets, but yes to inspired teachers and guides.

Many may start on the Sufi path hoping to become shaykhs, but very few attain the status of *wali*. It is the top level. The existence of such a possibility is enshrined in the Sufi view of the world, in its cosmology. It is not a matter of belief in the sense of an opinion; it is an understanding of how the world really works.

Shaykh Tahir-ul Qadri describes it like this:

> The source of spiritual bounties, kindness, compassion, love and affection is the holy personality of the most revered and exalted Messenger of Allah. To relay these vast blessings to all believers there are great conduits of Allah's friends who make up a spiritual power distribution system which works in a very similar way to electric power supply system... The *awlia* of Allah have vitalized and strengthened this 'conduit system' by their connection with our beloved Prophet."[33]

---

32 From Kabbani's introduction to Shaykh Nazim Haqqani's *New Day, New Provision*, Fenton, MI, USA Institute for Spiritual and Cultural Advancement, 2014.

33 Tahir-ul-Qadri, *Islamic Spirituality and Modern Science*, (London: Minhaj-ul-Quran Publications 2015), 113.

SUFI SCIENCE

Indeed, there is a whole science of Sufi cosmology. Ibn Arabi helped to systematise it. Sufism has always traded on the notion of restricted knowledge, that it is through personal enlightenment that the veils are removed and the believer perceives how things really are. For most of Sufi history knowledge of the spiritual cosmos was not widely disclosed. Today, in the global culture of research and publication, such things are written down and put into the public domain.

It is taught that at any one time, in the economy of God, there have to be a certain number of *awliya* present in the world. This does not mean that they are necessarily famous or even obvious. They can be quiet, secretive, holy people living in obscurity, known only to a few, but playing their part in allowing the mercy of God to flow through the world. The *awliya* themselves form a hierarchy. At the very top is the *qutb*, literally meaning "pole" in the magnetic sense, or the axis on which the spiritual world turns. Such a belief injects another level of intensity into the world of Sufi movements. Occasionally Sufi masters explicitly lay claim to the title. More often it is ascribed to them by their followers. For Rumi, Shams al-Din was said to be a *qutb*. One of the things that excites some Sufi followers is that their shaykh might be a true *wali* or even the *qutb* of this time. Kabbani, quoted above, does not use the word *qutb* with reference to his master, but calls him something that amounts to the same thing, namely *Sultan al-Awliya*, king of the saints for this time.

In many parts of the Muslim world, shrines built around the tombs of great holy men attract pilgrims and petitioners. The true *wali* is seen as never really absent. People come to express reverence and to seek help, in other words to pray to their patron saint. If we find echoes of the saint veneration in the Roman Catholic world, that perhaps tells us something about human beings and their desire to have a visible, tangible focus as they seek supernatural help. In fact, there is even a culture of relic veneration in operation. Sufi Islam denies any idolatry is involved, on the basis that no one is claiming that Muhammad or the *awliya* are gods. Nevertheless, praise and petition are directed towards them.

If all this seems weird and alien, it has credibility and power because it is not too far off the mark. It is true that God never intended people to depend on a set of written rules and regulations. It is true that he intends them to rely on a living presence. It is true that he calls and inspires flesh and blood human beings to serve him and to serve believers. The gift of the Holy Spirit makes this a reality. And there is a supreme King of Saints. Nor does God leave people without a witness. He calls us all to represent him to those that do not yet know him.

Sufism, politics and holy war

THE IMAGE BEFORE ME WAS OF HILLARY CLINTON and a beaming man with a Santa Claus beard wearing robes of a Middle-Eastern style. And it was not an alternative Christmas. I found an image of the same gentleman, all smiles, shaking hands with Prince Charles in London. Linked to these, I came across images and video clips of Islamic celebrations of Muhammad's birthday in the UK Houses of Parliament. I was researching the activities of the followers of Shaykh Nazim Haqqani. The man in the photos was Hisham Kabbani, one of his closest associates, who headed up the work in the USA.

Following 9/11 and the launch of President George Bush's "war on terror", Western governments started to pay attention to what was going on inside the Muslim community. Long story short, it was discovered that the Muslim Council of Britain, which up to that point was the main body that the UK government looked to as representing Muslim sensibilities, was dominated by a movement that looked back to the teachings of Maulana Mawdoodi, a fundamentalist thinker who was determined that Muslims should resist secularism and take their rightful place as the true servants of God ruling the world. Political advisers started talking about the Sufis as the voice of peaceful/moderate/non-political Islam. Various Sufi leaders put themselves forward. Haqqani's group pulled together an alliance called the Sufi Muslim Council in 2006, and they were courted at the highest level of government. Later, when the ISIS emerged in Syria/Iraq, many Muslim leaders, especially Sufis, publicly positioned themselves in opposition to that vision of Islam. Tahir-ul-Qadri published and distributed a *fatwa* (a ruling based on Islamic law) against suicide bombings and terrorism.[34]

NON-POLITICAL ISLAM?

Is it true? Is Sufism inherently non-political? Do Sufis reject armed conflict in favour of the inner struggle? Are they pacifist Muslims? If we look carefully, we find this is not quite what they are saying. It is what politicians want to believe.

Haqqani's movement was pragmatic and innovative in its engagement with the West. He preached against the evils that had free rein in the West, but also that his followers should not take up arms. Instead he said they should put their trust in God and stand firm, for God himself would soon send the *Mahdi*, who would tackle all the powers who were hostile to Islam. The faithful should focus on their devotional lives and on acts of service, leaving God to work out his plans for the world.

Cosying up to government authority did not start in the twenty-first century. In the Medieval period, once Sufis had become a significant presence in the Muslim world, rulers made them grants of land, and built them residences and training centres, much as kings in the West sponsored monastic institutions. Sufism was woven into the fabric of Islamic life, even if many of their teachers advocated a mistrust of worldly things.

Over time, in many places Sufi shaykhs came to enjoy many privileges and developed alliances with ruling houses. When political conflicts arose they were inevitably involved. When the Ottoman Empire collapsed at the end of the First World War, Kamal Ataturk refashioned Turkey into a modern-style nation. One of the first things he did was to ban all Sufi

---

34 Dr Muhammad Tahir-ul-Qadri. *Introduction to the Fatwa on Suicide Bombings and Terrorism*. London: Minhaj-ul-Quran International (UK), 2010.

organisations. One of the tensions in Turkey today arises from the fact that President Erdogan rose to power in partnership with a resurgent Sufi movement, the Gulenists, which he then turned against and is now actively persecuting.

ANTI-SUFI JIHADISTS

Movements such as al-Qaida, ISIS and Islamic Jihad are not just anti-West, they are anti-Sufi. For them, the call of Islam is primarily political and not about the interior life, which they see as a distraction. It was not hard for Sufis to align themselves with the West against the Islamists, but that is not the same things as a commitment to pacifism. They are often what is more accurately called *quietists*, people who distance themselves from corrupt or foreign government, but promote holy living in defiance of national norms in their own community. It is a sort of passive resistance. Armed struggle is not considered wrong, only inappropriate in the current context. This inevitably puts them at odds with the Islamic militants who want to mobilise all Muslims right now against their own corrupt rulers.

The word *jihad* means "struggle", and in Islamic law is associated with warfare to defend Islam. That doesn't mean it is only deployed defensively, since anything that threatens the wellbeing of Islam can in theory be identified as a threat, and therefore attacked. Sufis talk about the greater jihad and the lesser *jihad*. The greater *jihad* is the struggle against one's lower nature, the interior battle; the lesser is the battle against the enemies of Islam. Armed conflict is therefore not the main business of life, but it is by no means outlawed.

Islam is political. It addresses many areas of law and governance. Even those Sufi movements that have distanced themselves from government institutions – and many have – have done so for political reasons. Muslims expect Islam to have a powerful voice in the public sphere. In the modern West, religious belief and practice have largely been consigned to the private sphere and separated from the world of politics. We have no reason to expect the rest of the world to wholeheartedly accept such an approach. It is a manifestation of our own culture, not a universal truth. Some Sufi shaykhs operating today are teaching their followers to embrace this kind of arrangement but by no means all of them. Sufism has the resources to make this kind of shift, but it goes against the grain of Islam. Muslims are supposed to take an interest in how the world is being run.

In the tragic conflict that has been raging in Syria, we find some factions led by people schooled in Sufi traditions, other Sufi leaders who have spoken out against the government but not taken up arms, and still others that have sided with the government against the militants.

SUFI JIHADISTS

In the 2000s, when Western politicians were looking for suitable Islamic allies to counterbalance extremism, Dr Akhtar Injeeli, a family doctor born in Pakistan but working in the UK, became alarmed at this naïve approach. He wrote a book, published in 2012, entitled *Sufism and Jihad*, briefly explaining Sufism and its preoccupation with love and peace, but then documenting examples through the centuries of Sufis promoting and even leading armed *jihad*.[35] He might have gone further and looked into the fusion of Sufism and *Futuwwa* in the Middle Ages. *Futuwwa* had similarities to the culture of Christian knighthood in the Crusader orders such as the Templars. Young Muslim men committed themselves to serve God as elite warriors. The military training was combined with a Sufi approach to devotion and self-control, coupled with the absolute obedience required by the Sufi master. It was particularly widespread in what is now Turkey. This is not to say that Sufis are closet jihadis, only that Sufism as a whole does not absolutely reject armed *jihad* in all circumstances.

Sufis typically teach the priority of "loving the prophet". What happens then, when a conflict arises, not over territory or political policy, but in

---

35   Akhtar Waqar Injeeli. *Sufism and Jihad*. CGE Publishing.

the media or in literature? The mass demonstrations and book burnings attending the publication of Salman Rushdie's *Satanic Verses* in the late 1980s were not led by what we now call Islamists. They were led by the traditional Sufi-orientated Asians in the West. They were supported by Iran's Ayatollah Khomeini, himself an advocate of the Sufi life – unlike his successors. The book scandalised their intense devotion to Muhammad. For the same reason, the most passionate advocates of the blasphemy law in Pakistan are the Sufi-orientated, and some of their leaders have gone on record as sympathising with those who murder proponents of reform of the law.

Sufism does generally prioritise peace, love and harmony, and there are even strands that verge on universalism. But Sufism is also diverse. It is not a separate entity detached from the turbulence of the Muslim world. It is not the simple antidote to extremism that politicians dream of.

Born again Muslims?

THESE LAST FEW MONTHS I HAVE SPOKEN to many ex-Muslims, but that is not what I am talking about here. By "born again Muslims" I mean people who were nominal Muslims, then passed through a conversion-like experience, and have now become committed Sufi Muslims. People like Suleiman, a young British man of Pakistani heritage.[36]

Suleiman was in a state of crisis. The relationship with his girlfriend was falling apart, there was conflict in his wider family and he was deeply distressed. "I could have gone haywire. I could have gone both ways, but to be honest could have gone down the Islam way, probably become an extremist. But the thing is, I didn't. The shaykh came and he saved me."

In 2018, I had the privilege of conducting some research on conversion *within* Islam as part of an MA programme. I interviewed several people, all of whom were British-born of Pakistani background, and all but one of whom had been nominal Muslims. Some had spent their youth drinking and going out with girls. Then something had happened, and they knew they needed to get their lives sorted out. Each one submitted to a Sufi master.

---

36 This and other names in this chapter pseudonyms are used to protect the privacy of the individuals whose stories are being quoted.

I was investigating what it was that they had been seeking, how they understood their need. I asked them about what had happened, and how their lives were now different from those of other Muslims. In this study, I was talking to those who had signed up with Sufi masters from outside their own tradition, with shaykhs who were not rooted in Pakistan. In Christian witness, we should start "where people are at". I took this as an opportunity to discover how they expressed their awareness of a need for a saviour, and what sort of thing had convinced them that they had found one.

CONVERSION TO SUFISM?

The transition from the experience of Islam which my respondents had grown up with to the new path would be classified by secular sociologists as a conversion experience.[37] Most of my respondents went from being Muslim-in-name-only to reorienting their lives around Islam as taught by their new Sufi shaykh and as practised by the community of his followers. This would be similar in several respects to someone raised in a nominal Christian home embracing Christ and starting a new life, perhaps in a new church.

As Christians, we are perhaps accustomed to approaching conversion theologically. The needy sinner responds to God's provision in Christ, with the Holy Spirit playing a key role in that process. Since all people are sinners and we know that there is only one way of salvation, we may not be used to thinking about different kinds of conversion. However, looking at even Christian conversion narratives, we can easily identify three different types of experience. One is that of someone brought up in church, but who then, at some specific point, is born again. What is already familiar to that person comes to life in a new way; the new beginning is real and significant. We would also use the word conversion to describe someone with no religious experience of any kind who suddenly comes to faith in Christ. That transition includes entering new relationships and new patterns of life. Theologically,

---

37 Lewis Rambo, *Understanding Religious Conversion* (New Haven: Yale University Press, 1993), 2-3.

the same event has occurred, but humanly speaking the number of changes is considerably greater. Then, of course, we use the word conversion to describe the transition from being a member of a non-Christian faith to becoming a Christian. The changes that this process entails are different again, especially if the person was fully engaged in their previous religion.

Secular academics studying religious conversion from a sociological point of view recognise all these forms. Lewis Rambo has developed a widely used model for analysing religious conversion that seeks to identify typical stages. Rambo regards conversion as a process, and looks for seven stages: context, crisis, quest, encounter, interaction, commitment and consequences. The stories of my respondents exhibited all of these stages. Rambo's model proved useful in analysing them.

SEEKING SALVATION

I used a brief questionnaire about their experiences, followed by an interview so that they could tell their stories in their own words. My respondents had committed to three different Sufi shaykhs, each of a different tradition. The shaykhs they were following were Shaykh Mehmet (son and successor of Shaykh Nazim Haqqani), Shaykh Yaqoubi from Syria and Shaykh Habib Umar, a Yemeni. Not one of these three is based in the UK – all three were mentioned in chapter 8.

I had my respondents select from a number of potential reasons for committing to their shaykh. The reasons which scored most highly was "a desire for a more meaningful, personal certainty of God" and "the charisma of the shaykh". A "desire for spiritual healing" came close behind. The two highest scores are far from incompatible. The *desire for certainty* is met in a person whose *charisma* is such as to deliver that certainty. In the interviews, the respondents told their own story of meeting the shaykh, coming into his presence, and how their bonding with the shaykh brought them into a place of greater certainty, awareness and stability. The shaykh's personal charisma was a major factor.

Only one of the respondents had joined the Ba'Alawiya group. His account indicated significant differences in this movement's way of working. His pledge of allegiance was made to Shaykh Habib Umar, a man he had never met, the reason being that this shaykh does not visit the UK. Instead, his deputies or other senior members of the movement, speaking in his name, carry out the work. The fact that he committed himself without meeting the shaykh would also be true for many, if not all, of those that have joined the Ba'Alawis. The personal presence of the shaykh could not therefore have the same impact as for those in the other two movements.

Nevertheless, the charisma or persona of the shaykh's representatives was a key factor in his decision. The man he had most dealings with was Ibrahim Osi-Efa, also mentioned in chapter 8. What was true for all the respondents was that the desirable spirituality was embodied in real people, not in texts or other media. As this respondent put it in his interview:

> So, Habib Kazim fortunately comes to the UK… he will accept someone's pledge… on behalf of Habib Umar, and seeing Habib Kazim, he's a man who had a good influence on me… He seems very pure himself and conducts himself how I would expect someone of that ranking to conduct [himself]… And it was not just him, it was all the people and Shaykh Ibrahim being one of them and a number of other people that I have seen on this spiritual path,… that's the type of person I would like to kind of maybe become or be under.

The desire for "spiritual healing" scored very highly in the questionnaire. I was conscious that the term "spiritual healing" lacked definition, and did not correspond to any particular Islamic concept. Nonetheless, my respondents were quick to identify it as a valid term to describe their need. The interviews gave us a better idea of what they meant by it. Safe to say, it was clear that they were referring to a personal, individual need.

The reasons that scored least well in my questionnaire are also significant, family expectations being one. The follow-up interviews confirmed that family expectations were of minor importance. Not one of the respondents was following a parental example or recommendation in pledging allegiance to their shaykh.

"Dissatisfaction with previous religion" also scored low. However, since the subjects were not *abandoning* Islam but rather *finding a place within it that met their needs*, it is not surprising that they did not assign a high value to dissatisfaction. Their dissatisfaction was, in a very real sense, with themselves. They have not started attending new mosques; rather they have found out how to be Sufi Muslims in their home mosques by following a new path. They had come to a point of supplementing the worship in the mosque with attendance at regular Sufi gatherings elsewhere. In their verbal accounts the fact that they had been unable to find what they had needed in their mosques and parental traditions was very evident.

All but two described themselves as previously non-practising, and one of those two described himself as "practising but not fully". When they started seeking solutions to their issues, they did not find the answer in the norms of their local mosques or with South Asian shaykhs. For all but one of them, committing to a shaykh was the culmination of a process of seeking to engage with Islam as a whole. Although dissatisfaction with their previous religious pattern was not given as a primary reason for taking the Sufi path, it is clear that their previous religious setting was far from satisfactory, as these samples indicate.

> Rashid: I started going to the mosque and… at that time, there were no young people… You'd see just the elders. There was a complete detachment. I wouldn't feel comfortable and confident going to any of the elders to say, you know, could you help me in this kind of thought process.

> Salim: First time I ever met [the shaykh] and he's come out with some humour… and he amused the people around him, and I could tell it was to amuse other people, and I thought, wow!… You know, I went to

the mosque, there was no laughing and joking. When we were kids at the back we were told to shut up.

Suleiman: This religion looks like it's just for Pakistani people. You go to the mosque, all you see is Pakistani people and it's in Urdu, everything's in Urdu. There's no catering for anybody else at all, and I thought that was the religion.

The desire for a supportive community scored moderately well, but only one respondent gave it the highest score. The interviews made it clear that for several of them the fact of being in a community was highly valued, even if was not a major consideration in the decision to make the initial pledge of allegiance.

Hearing their stories from my own perspective, I noticed that what they had been seeking was to be found in the gospel of Christ. None of them were approaching their need from the point of view of being separated from God by sin, but all were aware of being alienated from God. They knew they did not possess what God intended for them. They all recognised their inability to achieve what was necessary. Encountering a person and a community that seemed to possess answers, they opened themselves up to new teachings, new practices and a new identity. True, there was no question of breaching the outer boundaries of Islam, which would have certainly raised the stakes for them enormously, but the fact remains that they were seeking things that God actually provides through Christ. They were willing to step away from family traditions to find what they needed.

THE ROLE OF DREAMS AND ENCOUNTERS

In the world of conversion theory, a pair of researchers called Lofland and Skonovd advocate the use of *conversion motifs*.[38] These are themes

---

38   John Lofland and Norman Skonovd. *Conversion Motifs*. Journal for the Scientific Study of

(not motives) that characterise different types of conversion stories. It is an approach that allows for the classification of the convert's subjective account, and many other researchers have found it useful. The six motifs listed by Lofland and Skonovd are intellectual, experimental, mystical, affectional, revivalist and coercive.

The intellectual motif describes the conversion of individuals through intentional private research, whereas the experimental motif concerns persons entering into the life of a group, behaving as though a believer before coming to a settled conviction. The affectional motif refers to the phenomenon of individuals being drawn to conversion by people with whom they have close emotional bonds, such as their marriage partner, close family or intimate friends. The revivalist motif relates to the sort of conversion experience which occurs in the intense atmosphere generated by a mass meeting or other highly emotive occasion. The mystical motif covers sudden paranormal-type insights or experiences such as dreams and visions. The coercive motif signifies genuine conversion that comes about as a result of the pressures of family, group members or imposed circumstances.

Lofland and Skonovd's original model presupposed that a conversion story would show one main motif, but subsequent writers have found it useful to identify different motifs at different stages in the conversion process, especially if the journey is long and conflicted. One person's journey may, for example, start with an intellectual quest and conclude with a mystical experience. In my research, I analysed the interview transcripts looking for these motifs without predetermining how many might be found in any one account.

For my respondents, the mystical motif was clearly dominant. For half of the respondents, dreams were a very important feature. The role

Religion 20, no. 4 (1981): 373–85. http://www.jstor.org/stable/1386185 Accessed: 27-02-2018 14:43 UTC.

of dreams was not necessarily the same in each account. One respondent reported that he had been learning from a variety of shaykhs over an extended period, but had never met his current shaykh or heard him speaking, before the shaykh came to him in a dream.

On the other hand, another respondent listed "mystical experience" as a reason for becoming a *mureed*, but in the interview he couched his whole story in terms of logic and reasoned decisions. When I asked about the mystical component, and whether dreams had featured at all, he looked a little awkward and said that he had received two significant dreams. I suspect that as a young man in a highly secular professional workplace, it was his habit to downplay the paranormal side in his daily discourse with outsiders. It was nonetheless a significant factor in his journey.

All respondents, whether identifying dreams as important or not, spoke of some kind of supernatural encounter in which some other power seemed to take control and direct them. This aspect carries over into their description of their life now as *mureeds*. As Yasin put it, "They say your shaykh chooses you, you don't choose your shaykh." Such a claim is one you would expect among Sufis, both among the traditional South Asian varieties and the newer international movements. The similarity between their experience and that of many Christians should not go unnoticed. Their words seem to echo those of Jesus himself in John 15:16, "You did not choose me, but I chose you." That experience of making a choice, but at the same time recognising that a higher power was bringing us to that point despite ourselves, is one that many of us can identify with. We will explore this further below.

In almost half of the respondent accounts, the revivalist motif was evident. Each time it came in combination with the mystical, that is to say, the key mystical experience occurred in a highly charged environment. In just one case, the highly charged moment was also the key turning point. For the other two it was an important step along the way that led to the decision. The mystical component was combined with, but not confined to, that episode.

The affectional motif appeared only twice and never strongly. In two respondent accounts the intellectual motif was present but not dominant. Their period of searching included some research of their own, but other motifs were also present and more significant. The coercive motif did not appear in any account, much as one would expect. However, it is worth noting that the *absence* of pressure to submit was explicitly remarked on by several respondents as something that influenced them. For example:

Suleiman: There was *no* emphasis on you to practise, there's *no* emphasis on you to follow or take initiation. You just come, you experience it for yourself... And I thought there must be something *real* here. [Italics reflecting the emphasis of the speaker]

Salim: Not once did anyone say that you must take allegiance or *bay'ah* or anything like that.

Muzammil: The environment was a very good – or for me – enjoyable learning environment, very chilled, very laid back, and it was easy for me to sit there and actually think, you know what? This is actually different to what I've got – of what's in my mind about how to become a practicing Muslim.

This is in implied (and occasionally explicit) contrast to the ways of their home mosques, and also to the ways of the fundamentalist groups that some had encountered at university. The value they placed on freedom to participate or not, to interact without being criticised, and to commit or not, came through in the interviews without being solicited.

Although the mystical motif is clearly dominant, the variety of experience should not be ignored. The secondary motifs show significant variation. One respondent conformed exactly to the experimental motif. He came across a Naqshbandi *zikir* gathering that happened to be using his local mosque and he was attracted to it. He participated in it for some years before seeking *bay'ah*.

WHAT NEEDS WERE MET?

The respondents were all asked what difference having a shaykh made to them. I asked them how they would explain it to a fellow Muslim who did not have a shaykh. The positive things they spoke of corresponded with the need for "spiritual healing" which they had listed as a primary reason for needing a shaykh. A sense of being connected to the shaykh was expressed by all respondents. All were asked how that works in practice when the shaykh lives overseas. For the members of the Haqqani group, travelling to Cyprus at least once a year to meet the shaykh had become part of their lives. While having that time of personal access was very important to them, being connected was not limited to those face-to-face meetings. They expressed to various degrees their consciousness of the shaykh being with them, aware of them, and they aware of him.

In terms of the benefit they found in being pledged to follow a shaykh, all the respondents spoke of having a guide. They spoke in different but complementary ways of what this meant. It is not so much that they had contrasting views so much as each one expressing in their own way the part of the overall picture that seemed, to them, to answer my question. They made reference to such things as decision-making, having a new framework within which to understand their faith, direction in personal development, and access to God. An appreciation was expressed for the clarity they now had in dealing with matters from an Islamic point of view, which came from a confidence in the knowledge possessed by the shaykh and all those close to him. The following quotes give an idea of the range of what is meant by being guided.

> Rashid: So, over the past ten years of my life, I can confidently say that any major decision that has been taken has not been taken without that consultation.

> Mahmood: The difference it makes is that having a shaykh, having a *tariqa*, you follow certain ways that keep you in touch with Islam, in

touch with your God… With Shaykh Nazim, he comes and says things to me in my dreams that I need to do. He may give me advice or may give me certain readings to do.

Salim: Guidance in the way that… you can change your views on things, for example, service and humanity. You can read all the quotes you've got about service from different people out there, but when I went to Cyprus I saw service, and I saw humanity was more important than the actual religion itself.

Suleiman: This shaykh has taught me everything – love, family, work and community, spirituality, friendship, children – everything.

Ahmad: It's like a guide, guide to God which you can't get in books. You've got books, you know, there's a lot of guidance in books, but it's the shaykh who has actually reached God and he can say, "Look, this is the way; come follow me".

Amir: So it's given me progression in the ability to serve, for example, but it's also developing me in my thinking, and what I consider to be important, and what I consider not to be important, and it's giving me some awareness about what matters and what doesn't matter.

Muzammil: If he [the shaykh's representative] is closer to God, he's gonna have a little bit more access. If I can get in with that person or we get a bond, and then that way we've got a chance of getting a closer – or we are going to get closer to God.

What these men are describing is a far cry from the standard representation of Islam as a dry set of rules and rituals and, in reality, Islam has always been more than that. Hearing these accounts from my Christian perspective, I found myself reflecting that what they desire to have is something that God desires to give them, and has made his provision for. It is Christ who brings the believer into right standing with God. It is through

Christ that the Holy Spirit is given, the ultimate connection to the divine. The gospel calls believers into mutually supportive communities. The head of those communities is Christ, who describes himself as the shepherd.

The Epistle to the Hebrews expounds how it is Jesus that meets our need. The first letter of John speaks of Jesus as our advocate. Because we are so quick to sum up everything in identifying Christ as God, we overlook the many mediatorial roles he plays for the believer. All the qualifications that supposedly give Sufi spiritual masters authority are found in the person of Christ in abundance. To put it the other way around, Sufi shaykhs are false Christs, pale alternatives to the real thing. The need which the research respondents felt for a relationship with God through a mediator is entirely appropriate, but they are not finding the mediator that God has provided for all mankind.

As Christians, we can identify with their sense of need, and we can see their shaykhs as poor alternatives to Christ, the saviour given by God. Should we conclude that we need to present Christ to such people as the supreme shaykh, the mediator and the guide they need? I think the answer is both yes and no. Yes, we need to present Christ as the one who connects them to God, but let us not overlook that they are desperate for a visible mediator and guide. The living, human guides they put their faith in actually point them on to Muhammad, the invisible guide, and speak as his representatives. In the case of the followers of Habib Umar, the local shaykh directs them to put their faith in one they have never met, but the local shaykh has a vital role too. Our inclination is to point them to our invisible Lord and encourage them to find him in a book. That is not the only way.

The apostle Paul used to say, "Follow me as I follow Christ". That's all right for Paul, but he was an apostle and we're not, we cry. Actually, what he applied to himself he also applied to others. Following the model of those more advanced in the faith was the norm in the New Testament; see Philippians 3:17, 1 Timothy 4:12, Hebrews 13:7 and 1 Peter 5:3, for example. That is how Christian discipleship is supposed to work, through people, not through books. The aim is always to bring the disciple on so that they will not always be dependent on us, but if we are afraid of ever letting people depend on us, we prevent them ever getting started. We need to see ourselves as representatives of the living Christ, not just signposts or book dispensers.

We have all heard accounts of how the living Christ has connected with Muslim individuals in different places through a mystical experience, usually a dream. The individuals I met in my research did not have that experience. They took the path they did because it was the one that was made available to them.

Sufi Mission

THE FOLDING CHAIRS HAD BEEN SET OUT on the parquet floor in two blocks of slightly curved rows with a central aisle. At the front, four chairs were set facing the audience along with some microphone stands, all ready as for a panel or committee. The venue was a rented community hall which had once been a United Reformed Church in a small town in northern England. It might have been a meeting of concerned residents or a minor political gathering. It wasn't.

There were about 40 people present, some in family groups. There were maybe 10 children. The majority were Asian but there were also about 15 White-British. The middle two seats at the front were occupied by a man aged about 50 and another about 30; we'll call them Mr A and Mr B respectively. The two outer seats were occupied by two young men in their late teens or early twenties. Mr B welcomed everyone and brought things to order. He was dressed in Western clothes with the addition of a green skull cap. This, he said, would be a time of mystical Sufi chanting. While such chanting may be a devotional practice for some, he assured us, it can also be a spiritual practice for all. Human beings were spiritual creatures. Participating in such an event could awaken our spiritual senses, easing the stress of life and bringing us back into balance. The words we chant, he said, have spiritual power. They are packed with spiritual significance right down to the individual letters. He encouraged everyone to join in, or at least to listen and imbibe the atmosphere.

One of the tee-shirted young men at the front took up a hand drum. Then Mr A, who was dressed in a splendid, decorated black robe and wearing a white turban started to chant in Arabic. The words were familiar to me: 'There is no god but God and Muhammad is his messenger' – the Islamic confession of faith. These are the words whispered into the ears of every new-born Muslim baby. These are the words that a person has to recite to convert to Islam. To the beat of the drum, the phrase was chanted over and over for about 20 minutes. The people chanted together, generating a warm, relaxed atmosphere. Many swayed gently with the words. After a while the words changed to such things as "He is living" or "He is almighty". After 40 minutes there was a brief silence, and then the microphone was passed to the other tee-shirted man.

Judging by his bulging biceps, he was well acquainted with the gym. In contrast to the turbaned gentleman on his right, he wore a blue NY baseball cap. His role was to sing a hymn. Many joined in the chorus, which consisted in the line "*la ilah illa Allah*" sung twice, meaning 'there is no god but God'. All the verses were in English. One included the words, "I am a raindrop; you are a raindrop… He is the ocean". This is a familiar Sufi theme.

The gathering was not over when the singing was done. Mr B told us that along with spiritual chanting, eating together was highly valued in their tradition. "People need community, and community is built round eating together." We were ushered into a dining area with trestle tables and chairs laid out and ready. A light three-course lunch was served totally free of charge.

FOOD AND FELLOWSHIP

The people running the event were followers of Shaykh Nazim Haqqani, and they made up a large part of the attendance. Where did the English participants come from? Some may have come in response to the posters dotted around town, but probably not many. Some had come from a local interfaith group that made a priority of being inclusive and accepting of others. Others had been recruited through the café.

Once a fortnight, this Sufi group takes over the pavilion in the park, and runs a "Friendship Cafe" for two hours on a Friday evening. Everything is free. People, they say, need bringing together. "They need space to meet and talk. They need community, and this is our contribution." The two buzzwords are 'spirituality' and 'community'. This is a clear and intentional attempt to draw the local English population into Islam. They ran such a cafe on Christmas Day, providing a full Christmas lunch to anyone lonely enough to need it. Those who enjoy this hospitality are invited to come to the spiritual chanting to benefit further. It is a well thought out and potentially successful approach to *da'wah*, that is to say, the Islamic equivalent of "doing mission".

DERVISHES WITH A MISSION

This group holds the chanting event once a month. Sometimes they have a special event and invite a group of Sufi musicians. One time they invited whirling dervishes. It was described as a workshop, not a mere performance. Here was a place to learn something new, to taste and see.

One of the visiting dervishes was a young man, probably in his teens. Frankly, he looked a bit awkward. The hat was tall, maybe 18 inches high, light brown in colour, and looking like it was made of something soft. He was dressed all in white. The outfit looked like it was made of old-style bed sheets, brilliant white and starchy, full sleeves, full skirt and white under-trousers. He looked like some kind of apprentice priest. Clean-shaven, his face was expressionless. His eyes were watchful, his lips remained sealed. He was not alone. There was a second person wearing a tall hat. His had a bright green turban tied around the base. This man was at least 50 and wearing a grey-green suit of a non-Western variety. He was good humoured, jokey even. He introduced himself as Shaykh A and he was visiting from the East – the city of Sheffield, to be precise.

On this occasion, about 50 people were present, half of them White British, perhaps seeking some kind of exotic spiritual experience, a touch of transcendence. Islam was never explicitly mentioned. The shaykh explained that although whirling dervishes were an amusement for tourists in some places, what they did was a spiritual exercise. Dervishes sought to detach themselves from their surroundings and focus on eternity. He got his young apprentice to give a brief demonstration of whirling, right hand raised, left arm extended, a little bit like the children's rhyme "I'm a little teapot." When he stopped, he folded his arms across his chest, palms on his shoulders.

The hat, the shaykh told us, represent a tombstone. The white robes represent a shroud. The folded arms are how the dead were laid out, back in the day. Awareness of death, he said, makes life more vibrant. The upheld hand represents an appeal to God. But this was a workshop, not a performance. So, who would like some lessons in whirling? Eager volunteers came forward. He had them stand motionless, arms folded, eyes shut, for some minutes. Then he asked them what they felt. Did they feel as though they had been rocking? Spinning? Holding steady? He then gave each one an on-the-spot interpretation of what their feelings meant.

Next, he had them hold up their right hands. One by one, he took their hand in his and gently adjusted the angle. As he did so he spoke to them. To one he said, "you need to be more decisive." To another he said, "you need to stop worrying about money." And to another, "you need to learn to relax more." Call me cynical, but I have seen the same kind of thing done by fortune tellers and mediums. Step by step, he taught the basic moves, each stage addressing something personal to the individual, drawing them into a place of greater trust. The exercise concluded with each volunteer rotating ten times while the audience chanted and clapped.

Then the host Sufi group performed one of their own rhythmic chants accompanied by a single drum while master and apprentice whirled before them. To complete the event, the usual communal meal was served. It was an outreach, and an effective one. It was warm, welcoming, relational and cringe-free. Mission does not have to be noisy. Nor does it end on the day. The event was filmed. Afterwards, a clip just a few minutes long, blending stills and movies and set to a soundtrack of oriental lute music was put out on Facebook and YouTube for all to enjoy. The participation of non-Asians was highlighted, including one man in a clerical collar. Then came the soundbite. One of the visitors, who looked to be a practical, working man with a strong northern accent, clearly responding to a question said, "I thought the Sufi chanting was very spiritual and uplifting. It is certainly something I would look into, y'know."

"GOOD NEWS" FROM THE EAST

I have described at some length the efforts of just one group. In the same locality, I have seen publicity for a group belonging to a different *tariqa*, one which practises silent *zikir*. They present themselves as 'The School of Sufi Teaching'. Hosting sessions every Thursday evening at the council-run Faith Centre on the site of a Sixth Form College, they describe their activities in these terms: 'A practical, dynamic and proven form of meditation that promotes a deeper understanding of intuition in the practitioner, and offers a profound insight into both SPIRITUAL and WORLDLY contexts' (use of capitals, theirs). The publicity goes on to emphasise the international scope of their tradition, and again in capitals, "OPEN TO ALL, IRRESPECTIVE of RELIGIOUS or NON-RELIGIOUS background."

Sufis are not to be found haranguing the public at Speakers' Corner, or aggressively handing out literature on street corners under provocative banners, but they do engage in missional activities. I think it is true that, as a general rule, they do not rely on preaching or persuasion, but on offering an experience combined with hospitality.

The British Muslim community constitutes a very mixed environment. The true Sufi distinctive is to be quiet in approach, to be self-effacing and to be non-confrontational. Rumi said "Raise your words, not your voice. It is rain that makes flowers grow, not thunder." More recently, I saw a Tweet in which Shaykh Tahir-ul-Qadri said, "Allah likes those who are soft-spoken. Speaking in a soft tone has been termed the best donation." This is advice to the follower, but it is also an indication of what sort of speaker might be taken seriously. If truly godly people speak gently, why would they listen to someone who is aggressive or assertive?

In many parts of the world, it has been Sufi shaykhs and their followers who have made Islam accessible to the masses of ordinary people as we mentioned in chapter 5. The emphasis on radical obedience to the shaykh provided a basis for leaving home to serve on the frontiers. The priority of experience and practice, rather than theory and doctrine, made their teaching accessible. Their readiness to deal with the invisible world of spiritual powers, a major pre-occupation in many cultures, made them relevant to local needs. Their master–follower pattern meant that they had willing servants to extend their work, and a visible path for disciples to follow. Their freedom to innovate gave them the flexibility to adapt to local conditions. Their readiness to embrace the local language, along with its music and poetry, gave their message access to the hearts and homes of ordinary people.

Shaykh Abdal Hakim Murad, also known as Dr Tim Winter of Cambridge University, was tweeted as saying, "If all Muslims were Sufis, then all people would be Muslims." I do not know what prompted him to say those words, but Sufis have been at the forefront of promoting Islam to the non-Muslim world for a thousand years.

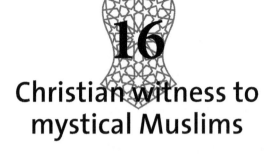

16
Christian witness to mystical Muslims

MAKKI (NOT HIS REAL NAME) WAS THE BLACK SHEEP of his family. His parents were respectable and his brothers were quite devout, but he spent his youth drinking and chasing girls. He led an utterly godless existence. Then, at about the age of 30, he got married and realised that he needed to get his life in order. He did not turn to his family, nor did he turn to his local mosque, where behaviour such as his had been denounced week in week out. He went looking for a man he had come across a couple of times while growing up, and who was now living about 40 miles away. This man was a Sufi following a Moroccan master. Despite his waywardness, Makki still had a Sufi view of the world. When his neediness came into painfully sharp focus, he went looking for a man who was quiet, wise and serene, one in whom he saw the signs of closeness to God.

Yasin was raised in a thoroughly nominal family. Islam was never more than a label for him or for them. He too spent his youth clubbing with his mates and battling regular hangovers. There came a point when he woke up in the morning knowing that this could not continue. He tagged along with a group of friends going to a conference on how to be a Muslim in the modern world and met a Sufi shaykh. He immediately recognised him as a source of light, a potential guide, a connection with the divine. It was a turning point. He now helps lead a local Sufi circle.

Both these men came to a point in their lives when they started seeking how to break free of destructive habits and find peace with God. What would have happened if there had been godly Christians in their circle of acquaintance? Would they have recognised the presence of God? Would they have seen the mysterious *something* that they knew they needed? Did they in fact know some Christians, but failed to recognise Christ in them? We cannot know the answer, but it is an intriguing question which cuts two ways. Firstly, could a spiritually bankrupt Muslim look beyond Islam? These two did not. They assumed that they would have to look within the boundaries of their inherited faith, but at the same time, they took a new and individual path. Secondly, do we Christians live and speak in such a way that those with a Sufi view of the world would know that we actually have what they seek?

FURTHER FROM OR NEARER TO THE GOSPEL?

Many Christians coming suddenly on the Sufi dimension of Islam recoil in horror. If Muslims in general are hard to reach, what about these Sufis with their dabbling in mysterious powers? It all depends on which end of the telescope you are using. Sufis may seem alien and disturbing, but if we look again in the cold light of day, we find some solid common ground with ourselves. In contrast to textbook Islam, and in common with biblical teaching, they know they need saving. They know that they cannot save themselves by their own efforts. Knowledge of God's laws is not enough. They need a guide, a presence, a power, to have any chance of obtaining peace with God.

With this we agree, though we might use other terminology and couch it in a different framework. The fact that the Sufi masters can be seen as saviour-type figures is evidence of an awareness of a need for a saviour, one who mediates for them. Not only is this need felt, but they hold a belief that it is God's will and intention that such a saviour exists. With this too we agree, for there is one God and one mediator between God and humankind, the man Christ Jesus (1 Timothy 2:4), and God has given no

126

other name under heaven by which we may be saved (Acts 4:12). They are looking for the right thing in the wrong place. Sufi-minded people look for a person who models the way, embodies the truth and is a source of life (John 14:6). As the writer to Hebrews bore witness, we have a high priest who meets our need, and who is holy and blameless (Hebrews 7:26). That he defeated evil, reigns over the invisible powers and has triumphed over death is foundational to the message of the New Testament. Jesus is not just alive in the grave yet somehow with us; he left his grave empty and entered the indestructible life of the world to come. He is present with his people by his Spirit.

We are not generally in the habit of speaking of Christ in this way to non-Christians. We go straight to his being the Son of God and/or being God. We get bogged down in attempting to explain heavenly realities in human language. The scriptures themselves do not start from this point. Careful sifting of the text and examination of the implications bring us to that point, but we so often start with the conclusion and we lose our listeners. The scriptures describe in much fuller terms than we usually do the many ways in which Christ meets the needs of the seeker after God.

QUIETNESS THAT SPEAKS

In discussing our message, we are already placing the cart before the horse. No matter how well-crafted our message is, it can do no good unless it is heard, nor will anyone listen unless we have credibility.

Sufi-minded Muslims seek quietness in a noisy world. The Muslim community has its fair share of assertive and aggressive preachers. Proof-texters compete for their attention. Sufis screen them out. Like Rumi, they are on the alert for truth beyond words. If they identify quietness and serenity as the authentic markers of one who knows truth, then traditional evangelical approaches are counter-productive. On the other hand, Jesus was described in these terms: "Look at my Servant, whom I have chosen. He is my Beloved, who pleases me. I will put my Spirit upon him, and he will proclaim justice to the nations. He will not fight or shout or raise his voice in public. He will not crush the weakest reed or put out a flickering candle." (Matthew 12:18-20, NLT) That is a very attractive image to the Sufi-minded. We need to be more intentionally like Jesus.

Genuinely seeking to follow the example of Jesus can never, by definition, be a compromise, or mere pandering to the foibles of a particular group. To be sure, our Western culture prefers clear unambiguous statements of truth addressed to the mind, but Jesus himself often spoke in parables. He imparted memorable stories and sayings, many of which did not confront but caused some listeners to come back for more.

FISHING WITH BAIT NOT NETS

Imagine a scenario in which a Sufi friend is saying how wonderful his experience is. You smile and say, "That is precious. It is like silver." That is an affirmation, not a confrontation. But it carries an implication that elsewhere gold is to be found. If your friend picks up on it, instead of a "what we believe is" response, you tell the story of the poor man digging in the field (Matthew 13:44). He found such treasure that he gladly abandoned everything he had to obtain it. That leads on to the parable of the rich man who collected pearls. When he found the greatest pearl, he happily forfeited everything to obtain it. You tell the story. You don't talk about us or them. You talk about the precious gift of God. You talk about the treasure that gives assurance of God's love and his powerful presence in the heart of the believer. Make them curious. Tap into hunger. Invite the question.

ISSUES OF ASSURANCE?

Sufis I have spoken to are not wrestling with what will happen to them when they die. That doesn't mean it does not matter to them, nor does it mean they never give it a thought. It just means that it is not their main concern. Using that theme as the definitive reason why they should put their faith in Christ is not going to scratch where they itch. They are looking for connection with

God and help here and now. Although we have developed the habit of reading so much of the scripture in terms of final destination, much of it addresses relationship with God in the here and now. To be sure, the Kingdom comes in fullness later, but we enter it in the present.

Back in chapter two, I quoted a modern Sufi hymn that runs, "If when I die my sins are too many, the love of Muhammad will rescue me." That is not saying exactly what we take it to mean. It does not mean that Muhammad's love for the believer is so strong that the believer's sins are disregarded. No, it is saying that because the believer loves Muhammad, he will experience the love of God coming through Muhammad in return, which will enable him to do what is right. But even if he does not do enough, the fact of loving Muhammad will see him through. It is the daily relationship of love that provides the measure of assurance.

I was talking to a Sufi leader at a public event. He was aware that I was a follower of Jesus, and wanted to speak in a way that did not exclude me. "The important thing," he said, "is love for the messenger. Loving the messenger, that is what it is all about." By "messenger" he meant Muhammad, but left it open for me to understand the term as referring to Christ. I did not argue with him. Instead I gently asked, "Is your love ever enough?" His face fell. "No, it is never enough." So I replied, "Well, I have some good news for you. It is written in the word of God, 'This is love: not that we love God, but that he loves us.' This is the key: to receive the love God has for us. That changes everything." He looked astonished. "That is deep," he said. But he did not ask more, and I did not press it. I have no doubt that those words have stuck with him. I pray that one day we can take the conversation further.

USING PARABLES

I have found that if we are put on the spot and asked to come up with a parable that might speak to Sufi sensibilities, many of us go to the prodigal son or the lost sheep. Yes, they can be given a particular relevance – the embrace of the father and "what you seek is seeking you" – but they are parables that particularly speak to us Western Christians. How about the vine in John 15? This is what God has provided for all who will believe. Jesus the never-dying vine into whom we can be grafted (a tighter bond than *rabita*), and whose life flows through us (a closer presence than *suhba*). How about the good shepherd? Or the hidden treasure?

CALLING THEM HIGHER

Most of us that seek to reach Muslims are aware that the term "Christian" has its drawbacks. To Muslims, it is more or less an ethnic or cultural category. Of course they don't want to "become Christians" – the expression carries no positive spiritual associations at all. They may want to be clean before God, they may want to be accepted, to be counted righteous and to live in the awareness of the goodness of God – all fruits of following Christ, but the term *Christian* is not associated with any of these things in their ears. For this reason, many of us prefer to describe ourselves as followers of Jesus, rejecting idols and worshipping God. On one occasion when we were prayer walking, I got into conversation with the leader of a local Sufi group. I said I was a follower of the Lord Jesus. "Actually," he said, "we Sufis love Jesus. He is a great model for us!" How should we respond to such a statement? Should we respond with polite hostility, saying that he did not really love Jesus because he did not know him? Should we answer expressing suspicion? "But do you *really*? Do you obey all his commandments?"

The answer only came to me when the moment had passed. It is not about knocking them down, but about calling them higher. Next time, I will respond like this: "I am delighted to meet anyone who loves Jesus! Isn't it wonderful what he promises to those who love him? You know what I mean?" This must inevitably leave him wrong-footed, but as one missing out, not as one being dismissed. Having stirred some curiosity, I would then either open up the Bible or simply quote John 14:23 – "All who love me will do what I say. My Father will love them, and we will come and make our home with each of them." What a promise! That God himself will make his home in our hearts!

While the use of the text takes the risk of opening up a reason-based discussion about Father and Son, it also imparts a powerful message direct to the hungry heart – "making our home with him." Sufis are used to figurative language, so the vocabulary of father–son need not be an immediate stumbling block, but this promise of intimacy with God should excite the interest of the sincere seeker.

TASTE AND SEE

In the previous chapter, we saw that Sufis doing mission tend to offer experiences rather than rational argument. That they do this is an indication of what they themselves respond to. We might argue that Jesus did the same. He gave them a sign in the form of a miracle, and then taught them. The signs got their attention. We had a series of Muslim-friendly guest services at our church. Very little of the format was changed to accommodate Muslim visitors. The effort to invite them had been made, they knew they were welcome, and the message was adapted. One of those who came was the head of a local Sufi group. He arrived a little late and had to leave a little early to collect his son from football, but as he sat at the back through the worship time, he quietly wept. "There is so much love in this place," he was heard to say as he slipped out. Was he saved? No. Was he touched? Definitely. He experienced a sign. He hosts his own outreach events at which no one weeps.

It is not a matter of concealing the truth; rather it is a refusal to use truth as a big stick with which to drive people away. People were drawn to Jesus because of who he was and what he did. He spoke to them in parables. He explained things explicitly to those that spent time with him and asked questions. There is a world of difference between force-feeding people who we think are hungry and letting the hungry get a whiff of the bacon.

THE BLINDFOLD

We should, of course, never run away with the idea that just because we understand where someone is coming from or just because we have learned some appropriate responses, that bringing them to Christ will be easy. In 2 Corinthians 4:4 Paul reminds us that the god of this world has blinded the minds of unbelievers. The thickness of the blindfold is increased for those who invest themselves in elaborate belief systems that bind them to mystical masters. Concerted intercessory prayer inevitably plays a bigger part than having smart answers in our back pockets. Without the active power of God there can be no progress. This also means that when someone responds to the Good News of Jesus and seeks to follow him, bondages will need to be broken through repentance, renunciation and the deliverance work of the Holy Spirit.

DISCIPLESHIP

One advantage that the Sufi-minded have over the rest of us is this: they understand what discipleship is. We may have our manuals and programmes, but they are a far cry from the practice of Jesus himself. Sufis know that discipleship is about forming a relationship, applying themselves to listen and to obey. They look to the example of the flesh-and-blood person before them to make sense of how they can follow the invisible Master. We too should be open about being followers, valuing greatly the benefits of having a living master to guide us. That would be a step in the right direction. The bigger question for us is whether we can be the disciple-making representatives of Christ that they need us to be.

If we are to be effective witnesses to Sufi-minded Muslims, whether they be committed Sufis or simply those who have a Sufi view of the world, we need to be aware of them, and be ready to befriend them. Initially, they are more likely to respond to what we *are*, as shown by what we *do* and *the way* we do it, than by what we *say*. It is by our fruits that they will know us. We live in an unprecedented time. Muslims are coming to Christ as never before. Let's be ready to play our part.

Good News for Sufis

BEFORE WE CAN THINK ABOUT proclaiming the good news to Sufis, we need to reflect on scripture for a few minutes.

Mark 1:14-15 tells us that Jesus went into Galilee preaching the Good News. What he said was, "The time promised by God has come at last! The Kingdom of God is near! Repent of your sins and believe the Good News!"

What was the "good news" that people should believe? What was the "good news" on account of which people should repent? It was that the Kingdom of God was near. For many of his hearers that was indeed good news, because they were waiting for the time to come when God would fulfil his promises that he made through the prophets, and finally establish his Kingdom. It was what they talked about among themselves. It was eagerly anticipated and discussed. When someone announced that the time had come and that God's Kingdom was near, that was unambiguous good news – so long as it was true, that is. They also had experiences of false hopes.

Jesus backed his proclamation with signs of the Kingdom. As he later said in answer to John the Baptist's question, "The blind see, the lame walk…" and so on, (Luke 7:22). People heard his announcement, saw the evidence and responded.

GOOD NEWS THEN AND NOW

Now, if you or I were to go out into the street and into the shopping centres proclaiming, "the Kingdom of God is near," who would think that was good news? Probably no one. Some might think we were announcing the end of the world and imminent judgement. Others would simply think we were crazy. No one would recognise those words as good news. The reason is that our context is different. We are not surrounded by people longing for the Kingdom to come. What made this news good in the first century was not that it was true (though it was) but that it was what people needed to hear. It is like if you saw an ambulance parked outside your house. If you were returning home unaware of a problem, the ambulance would be bad news. If you are inside the house with a bleeding child or a crumpled grandmother, the presence of the ambulance is good news. Same piece of news, different context.

If we skip ahead into Acts, we find the good news being proclaimed, but the words used by the apostles are different. In the early chapters, as the apostles preached in Jerusalem, the focus was on the resurrection of Jesus. They did not need to announce the crucifixion of Jesus. That was common knowledge. What they announced was his resurrection. For what reason? Because the raising of Jesus was evidence that he was indeed the Messiah, the Christ, the promised one. Therefore, the listeners should repent and believe the good news. What often escapes us is the meaning of the word Messiah/Christ. He is "the anointed one", that is to say, God's chosen King. The King in the Kingdom of God is the Messiah, the one promised, who will reign forever and usher in the fulfilment of God's promises. So, the message in Acts was still about the Kingdom, but the context was different, and so it was announced differently.

As the apostles moved further away from Jerusalem, they needed to speak of the death of Christ as new information, but the focus remained on the person of Christ, the saviour sent by God. In the few examples of preaching to non-Jews supplied by the book of Acts, the difference is more marked still.

What God has done through Christ is a once and for all event. It will never become less true. However, over time, how we talk about it, how we explain it, has changed, because the starting point of the listener is different. Specifically, how we commend it as good news to those who have not heard it before is something that changes all the time, because the hearers are different. I have seen shifts in the way the gospel is framed in my home country even during my lifetime.

When we find that people do not recognise our message as good news, it is often because we are expressing it in ways that are good news for us, but not for them. Admittedly, there have always been individuals who do not believe. In first century Judea, more or less everyone agreed that the coming of the Kingdom of God was a good and welcome thing, but not everybody believed that what Jesus said was true. A good news message is one about which the listener will say, "If what you say is true, then that is definitely good news."

WHAT MAKES GOOD NEWS GOOD?

When we find ourselves talking to people who are significantly different from ourselves, people schooled in a different view of the world, we need to work out how to present our message in a way which they can relate to. The alternative would be to re-educate them so that they can understand it from our angle, and some try to do that. Some even argue that before people can grasp good news you have to hit them with bad news.

However, no matter where we come to faith in Christ, we have done so within a particular culture, and that culture shapes how we understand, interpret and explain the gospel. We quite naturally conflate the absolute truth of the gospel with our particular way of understanding it, because that is usually all we have to work with. As we are increasingly encountering people raised with a radically different view of the world, we need to be ready to step back and re-examine the gospel from fresh angles. The gospel is rich and deep. Its core message can be expressed in many different ways.

Now we come back to the question, in what ways is the gospel good news for people with a Sufi understanding of the world? What is the headline equivalent of "the Kingdom of God has come"? We are accustomed to applying the term "gospel" to the full theological explanation of what God has done in Christ as it is unpacked in the epistles, which were, of course, written for people who had already believed and repented. They had already become disciples.

The *initial* message of good news is what draws people to consider becoming disciples. In the first century, the signs provided the evidence to back that message. In other times and places, careful reasoning has been more highly valued as reliable evidence. As Paul talks in terms of Jews seeking signs and Greeks seeking wisdom in 1 Corinthians 1:22. As we saw in chapter fourteen, the young men of Sufi orientation seeking after truth responded to experiences as evidence; in other words, they were sign-oriented rather than wisdom-oriented. This is also reflected in how they do outreach themselves. Who we are, how we behave, and evidence of the Lord being with us are really important parts of making our message credible, but we still come back to the question of what that initial good news message should consist of.

A ROAD MAP

I have hesitated to compose this section. I don't think it would be appropriate to supply a concise message to be fitted into a leaflet or blurted out on the spot. Jesus called us to make disciples, and when he made disciples, he spent time with them and enabled them to grasp who he was, step by step. This, I believe, is also the ideal for Muslims in general and Sufis in particular. Nevertheless, it does help to have in our own minds a "message road map" to work with. By a "road map" I mean a clear idea of where we want to go as the conversation or even the friendship unfolds. We have a strong sense of direction without being hasty to get to the destination. We watch and pray as our friend moves slowly forward, or to put it another way, as we see the Lord begin to open their heart.

At its simplest, it goes like this. God created us so that we might know him and love him. Since we cannot truly know him simply by our own efforts, he has provided the perfect intermediary, Jesus the Messiah, the living Word of God, the fulfilment of God's promises to the prophets.

The starting point, that God created the world and created us so that he would be known and loved, is one that Sufism teaches. What it implies for Sufis is less than it implies for us. We can spell it out and go beyond their expectations. God created us to know him and love him, to know that he knows us, and to experience his love for us. His desire is that we live in the awareness of his presence and that we hear his voice. Yet few people do.

We might take this further by unpacking what prevents us from knowing him. What is it that causes us to drift off so easily? Lack of true knowledge is a part, but that is not the full cause. The old formula which they recognise is the world, the flesh and the devil. Forces arrayed against our best efforts and our human nature, our ego, our *nafs* (as they would say), that draws us away from knowing God as we should. Consider the story of Adam. Though he lived in close relationship with God, he was tempted and he disobeyed, and his disobedience led to him living at greater distance from God. Even though God showed him kindness (providing better clothing), nevertheless his situation changed. If one single act of disobedience can cause this, how is it for us? Our experience of God is less than his was, our exposure to the world and the devil is much greater. Each failure to follow the will of God adds, as it were, to our debt.

We need three things: forgiveness of our debt, purification of our hearts and power to live in a way pleasing to God. All three are found in the Messiah, who himself never needed to ask forgiveness, unlike any prophet, never needed to be purified, for he was born pure, and by his word and his touch he purified those who were unclean, and he gives his Spirit to those who entrust themselves to him so that they may live a new life.

We can speak powerfully about Jesus without being forceful. We can speak about him in a way that invites people to join the dots. Even when they say, "Do you mean Jesus?" we can continue to be indirect as they work it out. For example, on his mother's side, he had nine men named in the Qur'an as prophets of God. On his father's side, he is "the word from God". He brings a knowledge of God like no other. No angel instructed him. Satan fled before him. The eyes of the blind and the ears of the deaf were opened. The lame walked, and dead people returned to life. Even his physical body is in heaven. His presence is with those who make *bay'ah* with him, to speak to them and to guide them. He described himself as the true vine. Those that join themselves to him become like branches, sharing his life.

Or perhaps more like this: God created the world so that he could be known and loved. God cannot be known unless he reveals himself. We cannot, by our own initiative, penetrate the veils. We can only truly know God as he wishes us to know him, if he takes the initiative. Here is a mystery, an ancient secret. Because of his great love and mercy towards mankind, God has entered his creation, veiled in human flesh. There is nothing that God cannot do. Though the world was made by him, the people of the world did not recognise him. Those who thought themselves to be learned did not accept him, those who were proud of their position and power rejected him. It was the humble and the needy who were enabled to know him. The true light came into the world, but many loved darkness. Men still construct ingenious arguments against him. His touch brought healing to the sick. The blind saw, the deaf heard, the lame walked, the dead rose. Sinners abandoned their wicked ways. He declared that he was the way, the truth and the life. Seek him and you will find him.

Or with a more explicitly Islamic flavour: They say holy men die before they die. What of the one who was resurrected before the resurrection? He is the Messiah. The Qur'an says, "they did not kill him," and certainly their boast that they had killed him was a lie, for his death was according to the plan of God that he might be the first of the resurrection. He is the living one who gives life. He is the Second Adam, the Heir of Abraham and the Son of David. He holds the keys of life and death. He is alive and active.

It has become common in the West to make the cross central to the message, and to major on explanations of how it works and why it was necessary. We speak of it as the place where a transaction was made leaving nothing for us to do. The freeness of God's grace is good news to us, but the scriptures actually say so much more. Sufis want to hear about what the grace of God produces.

We may want to hear that we can get off scot free, but they want to hear how the greatness of God's love bridged the gap, and how he provided a saviour who leads and guides. The incarnation of Christ, death as a sacrifice, his glorious resurrection, his ascension to the right hand of power, and the giving of the Holy Spirit are all important elements of salvation. We need to let God teach us how to unpack the mysteries of the truth in the way that most helps our listener, not just the way that most resonates with us.

Epilogue

"THE APPROACH WE USE FOR ORDINARY MUSLIMS slips off their [the Sufis'] souls without touching them in the least; whereas read them a few pages of John's Gospel or one of the epistles and there is a response at once... It seems strange that hardly a thing has been written for them or much thought given to them..."

These words were written by Lilias Trotter in her diary on 9th July, 1923.[39]

Lilias Trotter, a young English woman from a privileged background, arrived in Algeria in 1888. The country had been under French rule since 1830 and the population was very conscious of being colonised by an unfriendly foreign power. She and her remarkable band of pioneers laboured in the face of resistance and hostility in the city of Algiers. In 1902, she and some of her companions had travelled south to the desert town of Tolga and come across a Sufi-dominated community. She was amazed at the warmth of the reception they received from the people, and she very much wanted to stay, but the authorities ordered them to leave. Twenty years later, she finally managed to go back again. She was

39 Quoted from Patricia St John, *Until the Day Breaks. The Life and Work of Lilias Trotter*. Bromley, UK: OM Publishing, 1990, 184 and Miriam Huffman Rockness, *A Passion for the Impossible. The Life of Lilias Trotter*. Grand Rapids: Discovery House Publishers, 2003, 289.

fascinated by the difference between the Muslims of Algiers and the Sufi communities in the desert.

In her diary entry, she went on to say, "Of all the millions of Islam, they are far and away the truest seekers after God, although in a weird and dangerous way." She described their prayers, their practice of *zikir*, and their belief that every human spirit comes into the world hidden in veils of darkness and light. On the one hand, she was concerned about their use of occult sciences, but on the other she said, "[their way] has a phraseology of its own which is far better suited to Christianity than to the religious language of Islam."[40]

What she seemed to be describing was a community much more concerned with the true knowledge of God than with the contested boundaries between the "Christian world" and the "Muslim world" which was such an issue in the coastal areas. She was invited to speak to students in the mosque, saw shaykhs reading the New Testament with their students and people putting their faith in Christ.

She was not able to stay long, less than a year, but the thought that "hardly a thing has been written for them" remained with her. She embarked on a programme of study and writing, which she pursued even while she was ill. In 1925, she completed a booklet in Arabic with the title "The Way of the Sevenfold Secret." It was addressed to the Sufi-minded, and based on the seven "I am" statements of Jesus in the Gospel of John. It spoke of the things that the Sufis she met were seeking. It was taken up by others, and almost immediately translated into other languages and distributed across the Muslim world. Today it is downloadable from the internet as a PDF document, free of charge.

What lesson should we draw from this story? I think it would be a mistake to seize on the *Sevenfold Secret* as "the answer", the magic key to

---

40   St John, *Until the Day Breaks*, 185.

unlock every door. The Sufi world is diverse and changing. The lesson we should learn from Lilias Trotter is that we need to be ready to learn new approaches specifically adapted to the Sufi-minded, and to speak in terms that correspond with what the people we meet are seeking.

The comment she made nearly one hundred years ago, that hardly any thought has been given to Sufi Muslims, remains true to this day. Very little has been written by Christians either for Sufis or about them, though perhaps this is beginning to change. More articles are appearing these days in missiology journals, and the book *Margins of Islam* includes pieces written about ministry to Sufis in several different settings.[41]

Perhaps God's time has come for a movement to Christ from Sufi Islam.

---

41 *Margins of Islam*, 2018, edited by Gene Daniels & Warrick Farah. Pasadena: William Carey Publishing.

Glossary

UNFAMILIAR TECHNICAL TERMS

Awliya	Plural of wali, see below.
Ba'Alawiya	A Sufi tariqa based in Yemen.
Baraka	Benign impersonal power channelled by holy men and women.
Barelvi	Name given to the Sufi-minded Muslim organisations in Pakistan, India and their migrant communities.
Bay'ah	Oath of allegiance by which a Muslim becomes a devoted follower of a Sufi master.
Da'wah	Invitation, especially the invitation to embrace Islam. Shorthand for Muslim mission.
Dajjal	The Anti-Christ, an evil end times figure in Islamic eschatology.
Deen	Religion, especially the required practices.
Deobandi	Name given to style of Islam originating in India which is devout, reformist and somewhat puritanical. Deobandis are often deeply suspicious of Sufism.

Dervish   Turkish and Persian word for a Sufi disciple.

Futuwwa   Manly virtue, especially in connection with commitments to godly combat.

Hadeeth   Accounts of the deeds and words of Muhammad from the early days of Islam, first passed on orally, later written down in huge collections.

Habib   Arabic word meaning "beloved." Used as an honorific title by some Sufi groups.

Hadra   Large-scale meeting featuring chanting and movement.

Ihsan   The perfection of faith, the basis for seeking personal knowledge of God.

Ilm   Knowledge, especially book-based learning.

Imam   Leader, especially the person who leads prayer in the mosque.

Iman   Faith, especially the articles of faith.

Juloos   Religious procession, most often to celebrate Muhammad's birth.

Jihad   Struggle.

Ma'arifa   Personal, experiential knowledge, as opposed to knowledge learned from books.

Mahdi   The Rightly Guided One, a figure expected to appear in the end times before the coming of Christ.

Mureed   Devoted disciple committed to obey a shaykh.

Na't   Devotional song.

Nafs   Soul, ego, the lower self, which is in conflict with the will of God.

Naqshbandiyya	A Sufi network originating in Central Asia.
Nasheed	Devotional song or poem.
Pir	Term used for a Sufi shaykh in Persian and Urdu.
Qawwali	The practice of professional devotional singing in the Indian Subcontinent.
Qutb	Literally, pole or axis: a holy person functioning as the centre of divine blessing, or a conduit of divine mercy in the world.
Rabita	Bond, the tie between followers and their masters.
Sajjad Nashin	The biological descendants of Sufi shaykhs who inherit their role and their baraka.
Salafi(st)	A radical, reforming expression of Islam claiming to be returning to original.
Sama'	Listening, used particularly in relation to practices of meditation with music and dance.
Seera	Biography of Muhammad, usually written with devotional intent.
Shadhiliya	A Sufi tariqa originating in North Africa.
Shaykh	Sufi master.
Silsila	Chain, the spiritual lineage of a Sufi master.
Suhba	Keeping company, especially spending time in the presence of a Sufi master.
Surah	Chapter of the Qur'an.
Tariqa	Way, path and, in this context, an organised Sufi movement.

Tasawwuf   The Arabic term for Sufism.

Wahabi(sm)   The form of Islam promoted in Saudi Arabia, generally
                    seen as opposed to all forms of Sufism. The word
                    Wahabi is often used as a term of abuse.

Wali   Friend, associate. In Sufism, a great holy person is seen
                    as Wali Allah, a friend of God, often rendered 'saint'.

Wird   Litany, order of worship, prescribed by a Sufi master for
                    his followers.

Zikir   Remembrance, practices of meditation such as chanting
                    to enhance awareness of God.

Finding out more.

Stafford Allen, **My Muslim Neighbour. Communicating Well with your Muslim friend.** (Gilead Books, 2016)
The best book around about Christians befriending Muslim people and sharing Christ with them.

Steve Bell, **Gospel for Muslims. Learning to read the Bible through eastern eyes.** (Authentic, 2012)
Presenting the good news in ways culturally appropriate for Muslims.

Ron Geaves and Theodore Gabriel (Editors). **Sufism in Britain** (Bloomsbury, 2014)
A secular book containing essays from a variety of academics about different expressions of Sufism in Britain.

Bill Musk. **The Unseen Face of Islam. Sharing the Gospel with ordinary Muslims.** (Monarch, 2003)
A classic, exploring the spiritual universe of ordinary Muslims across the world.

Gene Daniels & Warrick Farah (Editors). **Margins of Islam. Ministry in Diverse Muslim Contexts.** (William Carey Publishing, 2018)
A collection of essays by Christian cross-cultural workers in a variety of different settings some of whom talk about Sufism.

To listen to a variety of Sufi shaykhs speaking in English not only about Sufism and about other subjects from a Sufi perspective, the following can easily be found on the internet:

Hamza Yusuf, Tim Winter (aka Abdal Hakim Murad), Tahir-ul-Qadri, Muhammad al-Yaqoubi, Hicham Kabbani, Faizal Hamid Abdur Razak, Ibrahim Osi-Efa, Yahya Rhodus.

Because most of these will be speaking with a Muslim audience in mind, their speech will be peppered with expressions and vocabulary that is unfamiliar to an outsider.

For more resources please try https://thehigherpath.co.uk